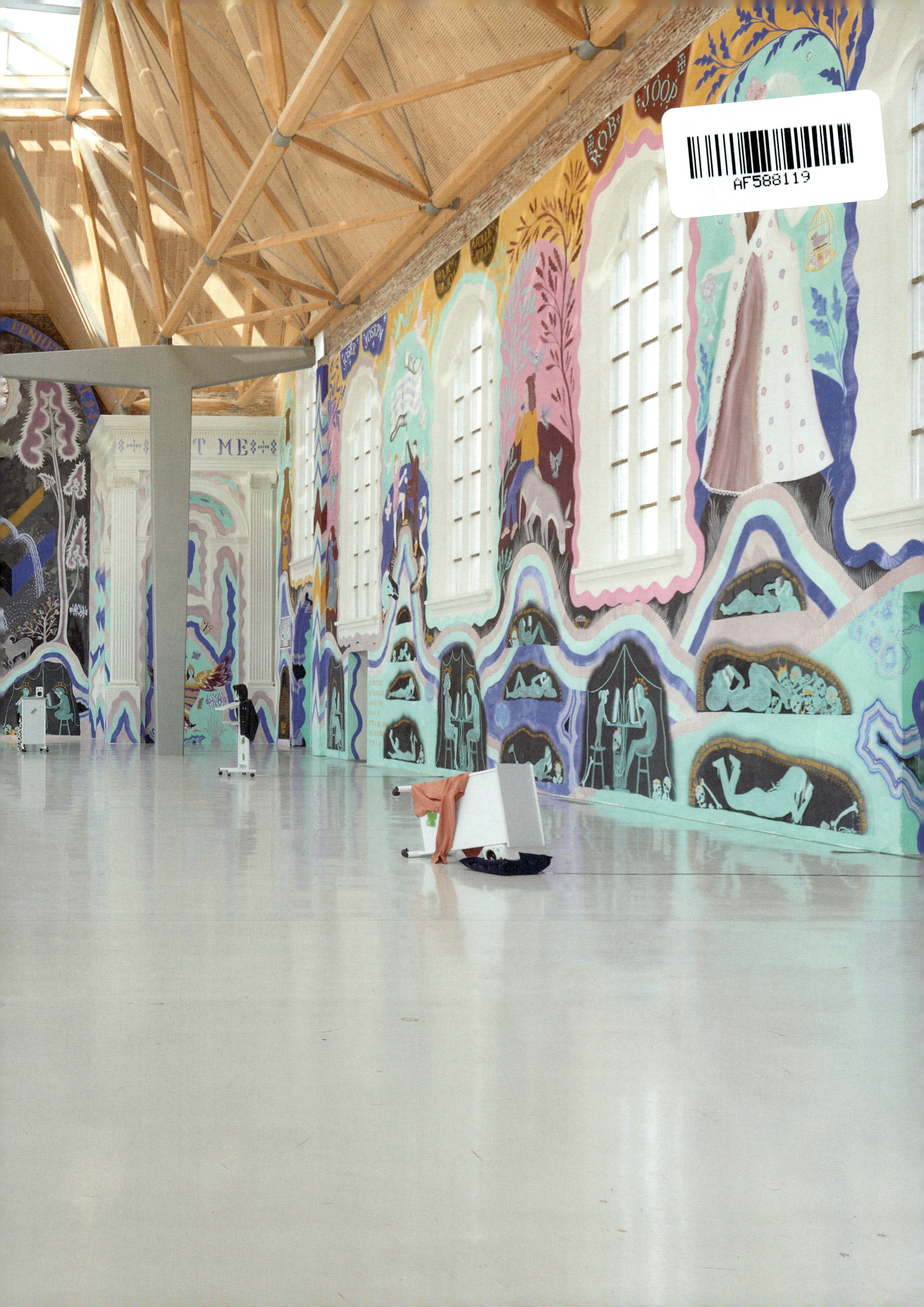
ROB
JOOS
T ME

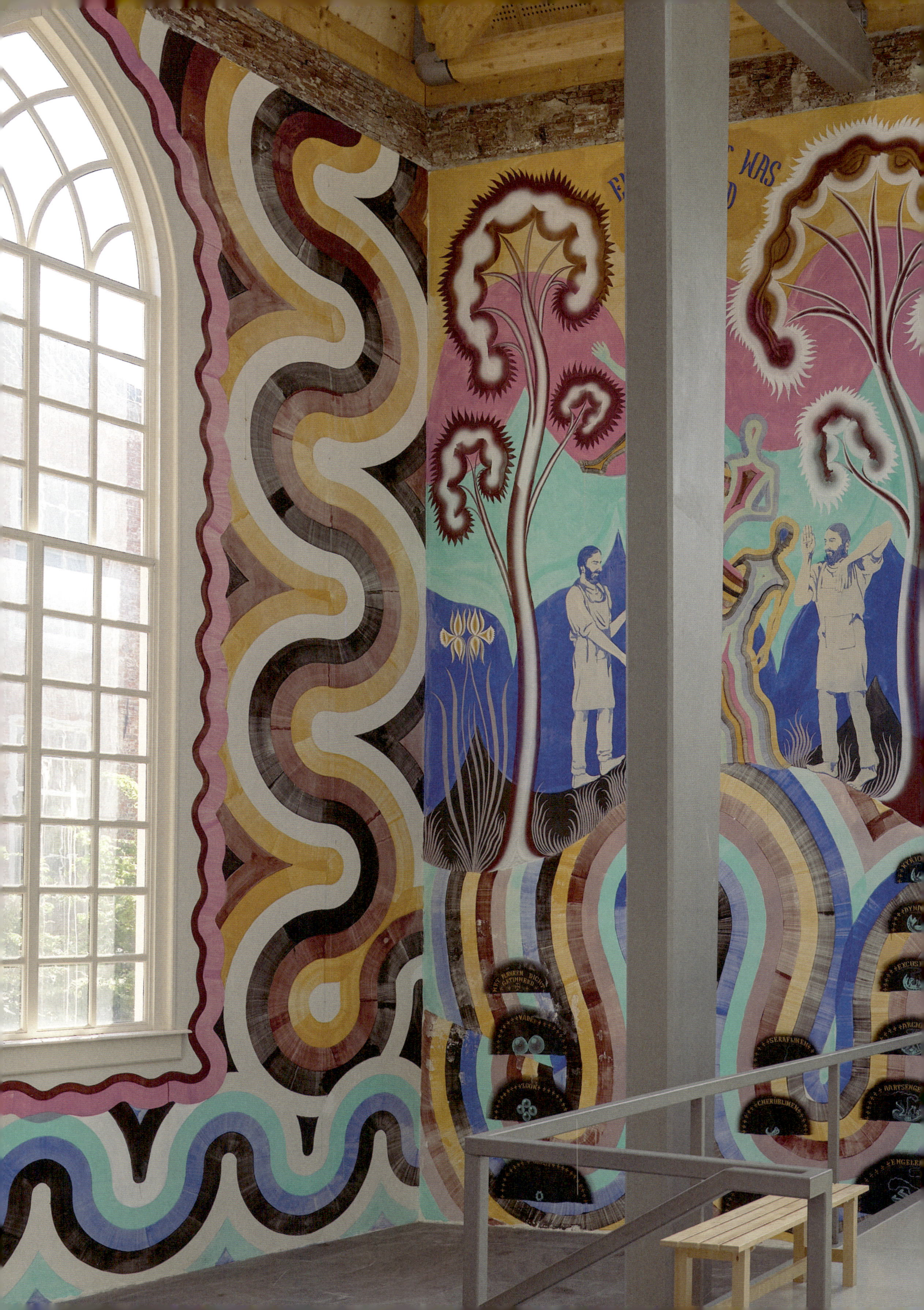
WAS
MET PLANKEN DICHT GETIMMERD
ZOON
SERAFIJNEN
CHERUBIJNEN

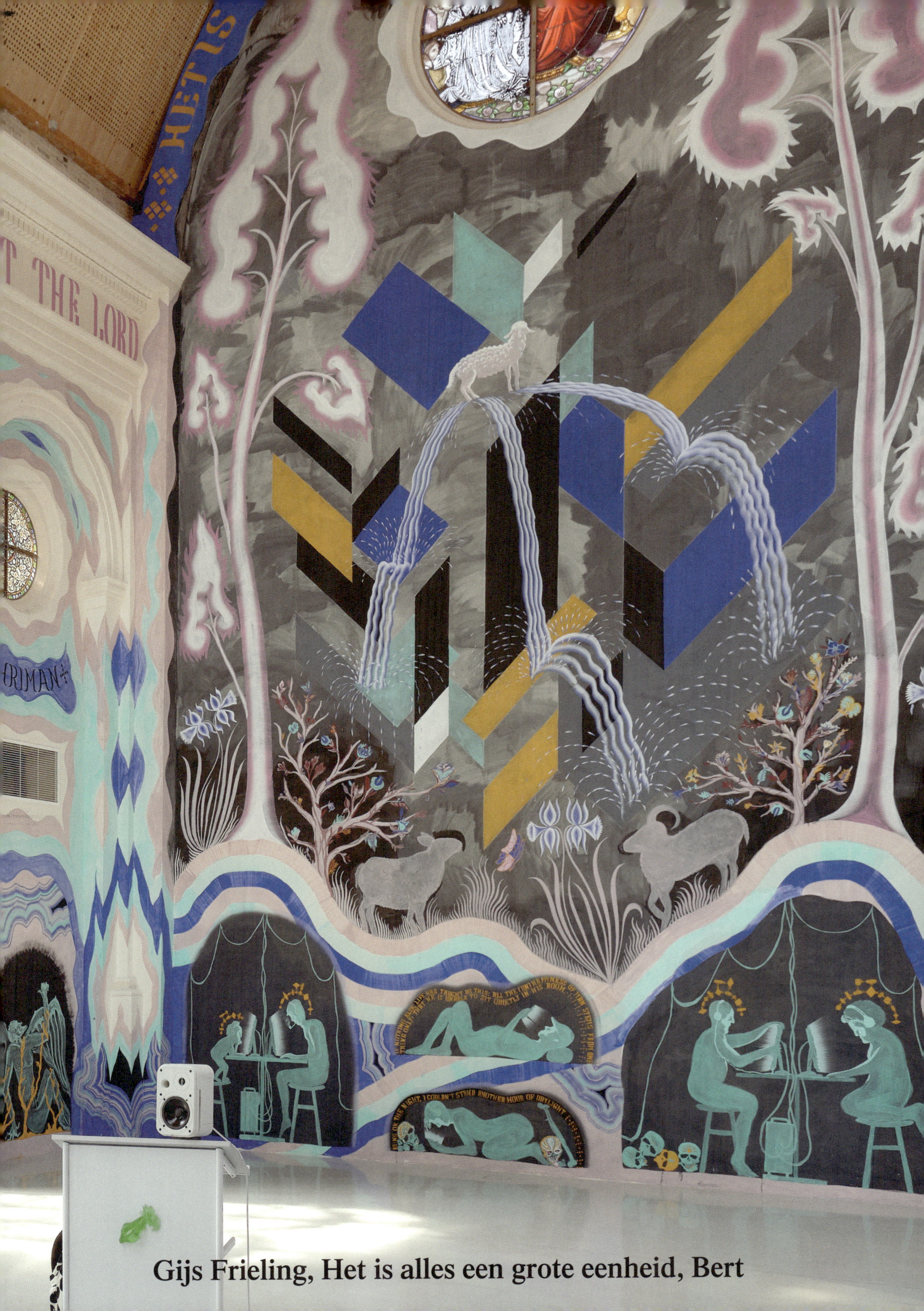

Gijs Frieling, Het is alles een grote eenheid, Bert

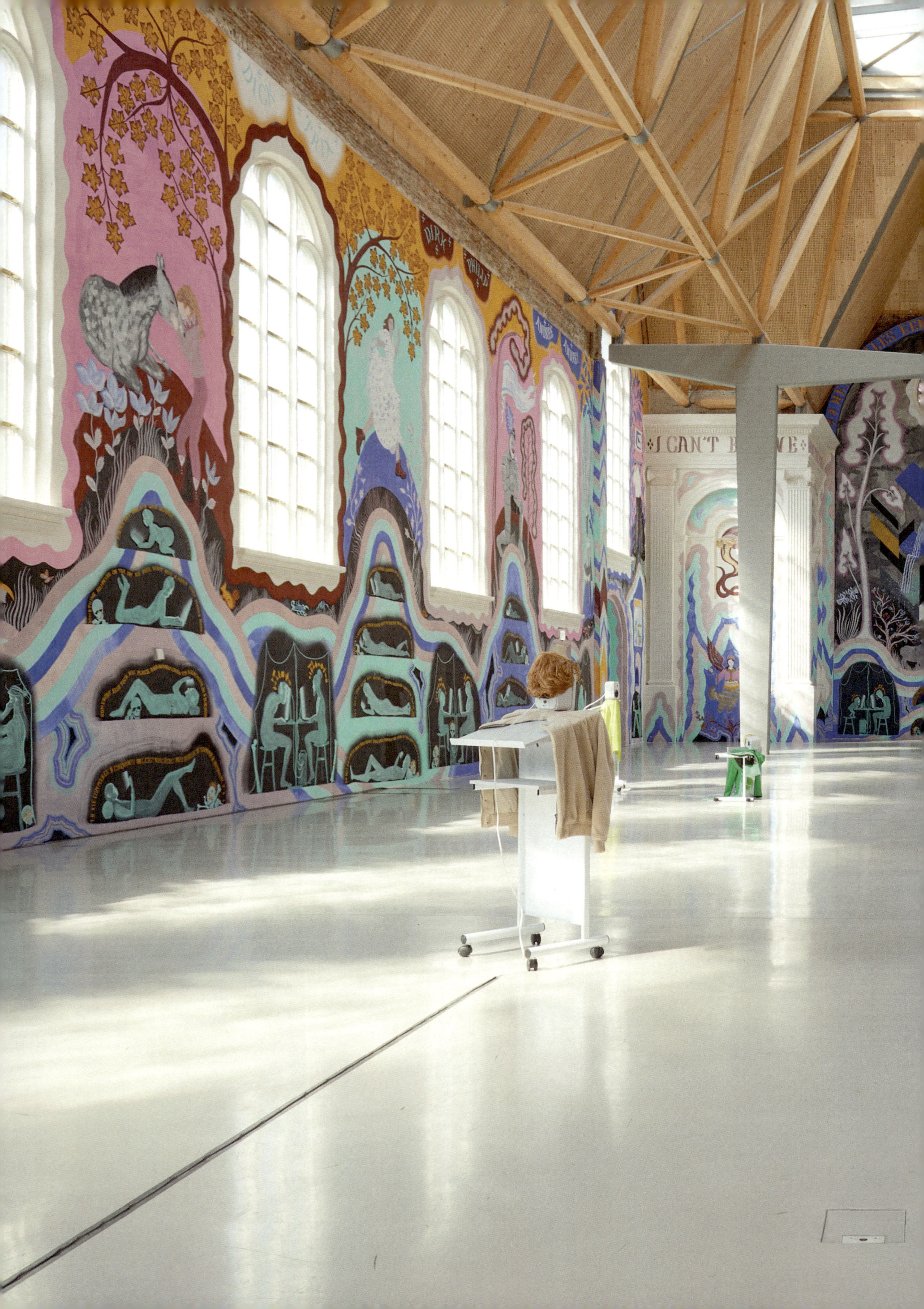

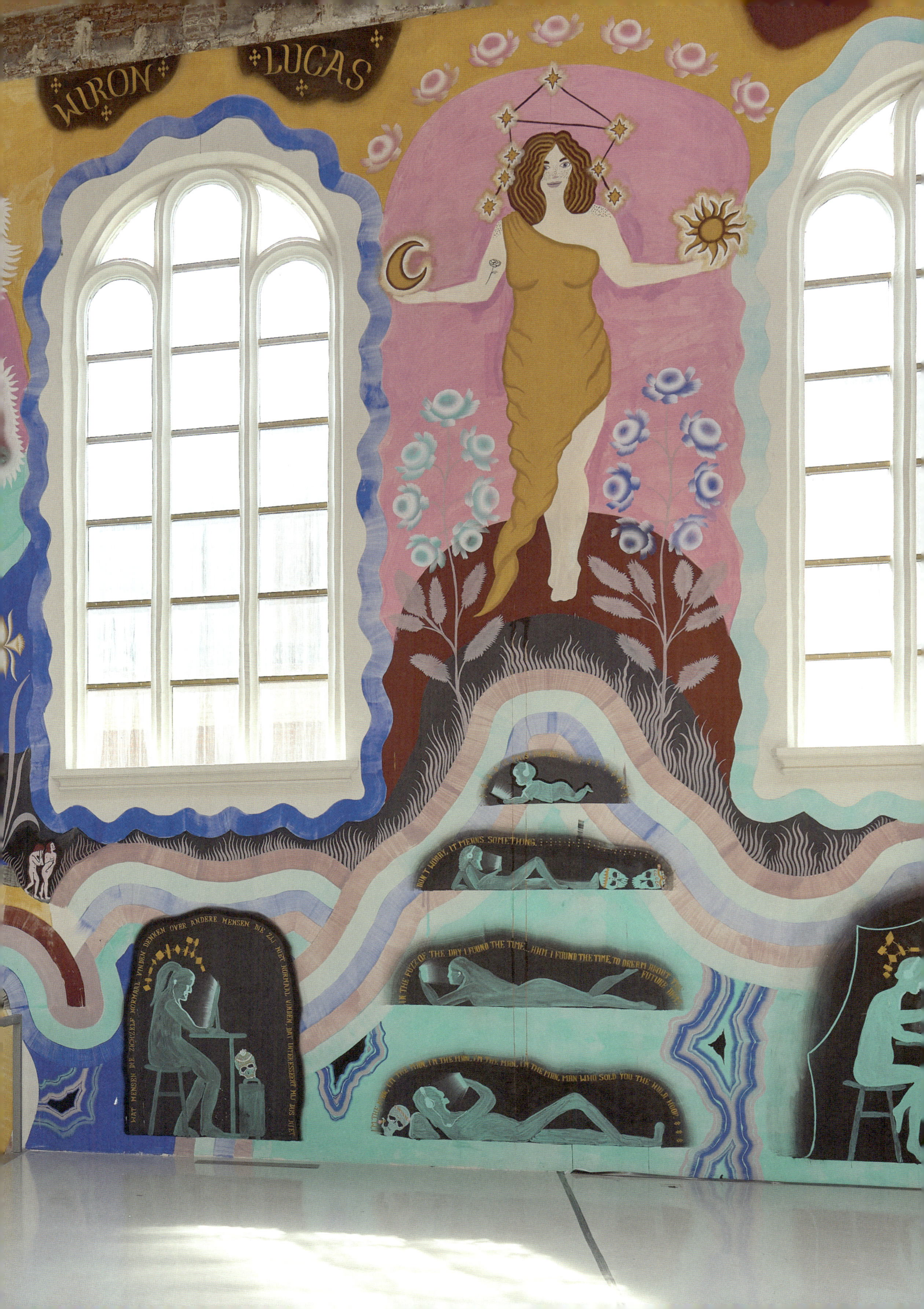
MIRON
LUCAS
DON'T WORRY, IT MEANS SOMETHING.
IN THE FUZZ OF THE DAY I FOUND THE TIME... AHH I FOUND THE TIME, TO DREAM ABOUT
FUTURE
I'M THE MAN, I'M THE MAN, I'M THE MAN, I'M THE MAN, MAN WHO SOLD YOU THE HULA HOOP.
WAT MENSEN DIE ZICHZELF NORMAAL VINDEN DENKEN OVER ANDERE MENSEN DIE ZIJ NIET NORMAAL VINDEN, DAT INTERESSEERT MIJ DUS NIET

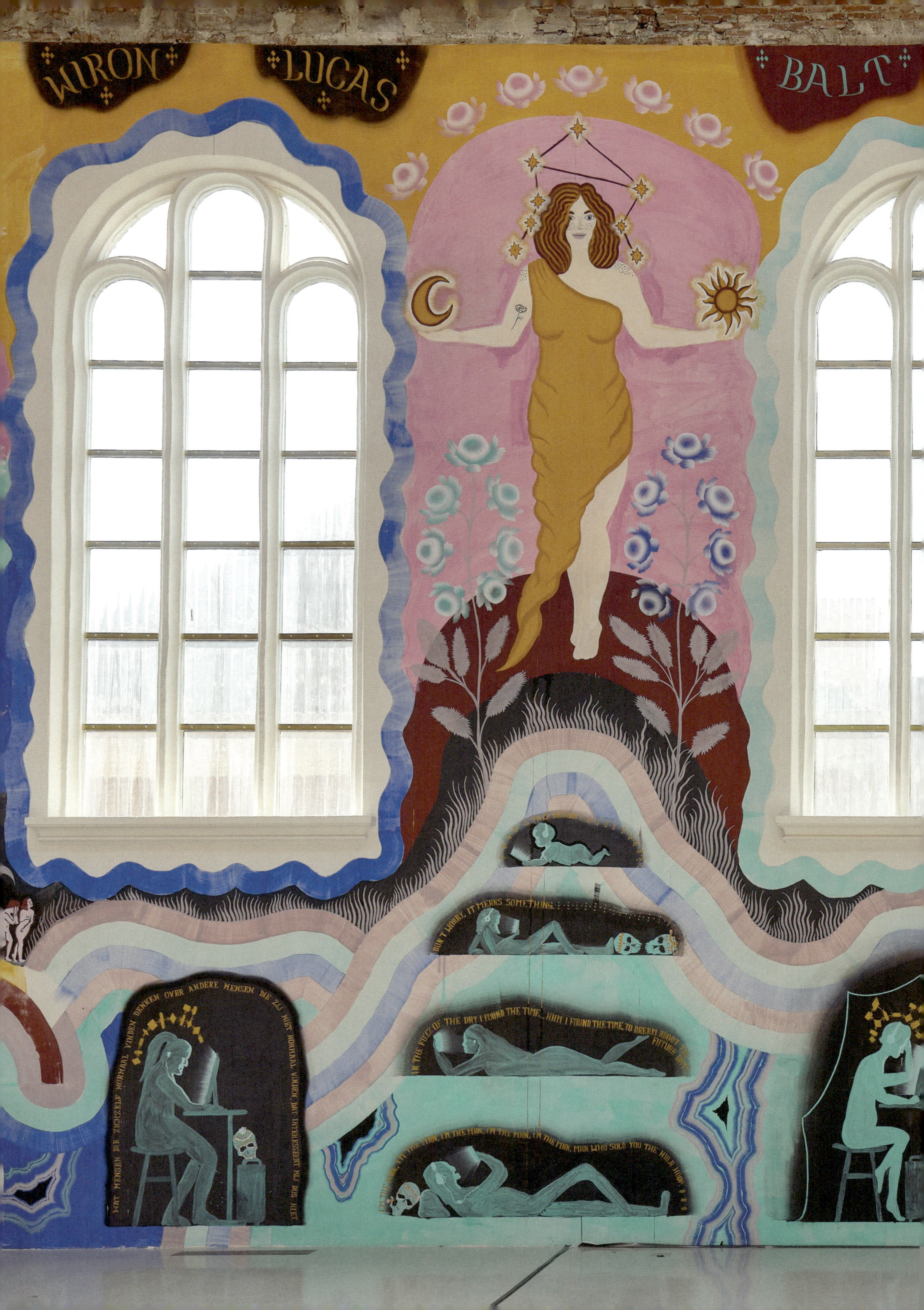
WIRON
LUCAS
BALT
DON'T WORRY, IT MEANS SOMETHING.
IN THE FUZZ OF THE DAY I FOUND THE TIME... AHH I FOUND THE TIME TO DREAM ABOUT
FUTURE DAYS
I'M THE MAN, I'M THE MAN, I'M THE MAN, MAN WHO SOLD YOU THE HULA HOOP
WAT MENSEN DIE ZICHZELF NORMAAL VINDEN DENKEN OVER ANDERE MENSEN DIE ZIJ NIET NORMAAL VINDEN, DAT INTERESSEERT MIJ DUS NIET

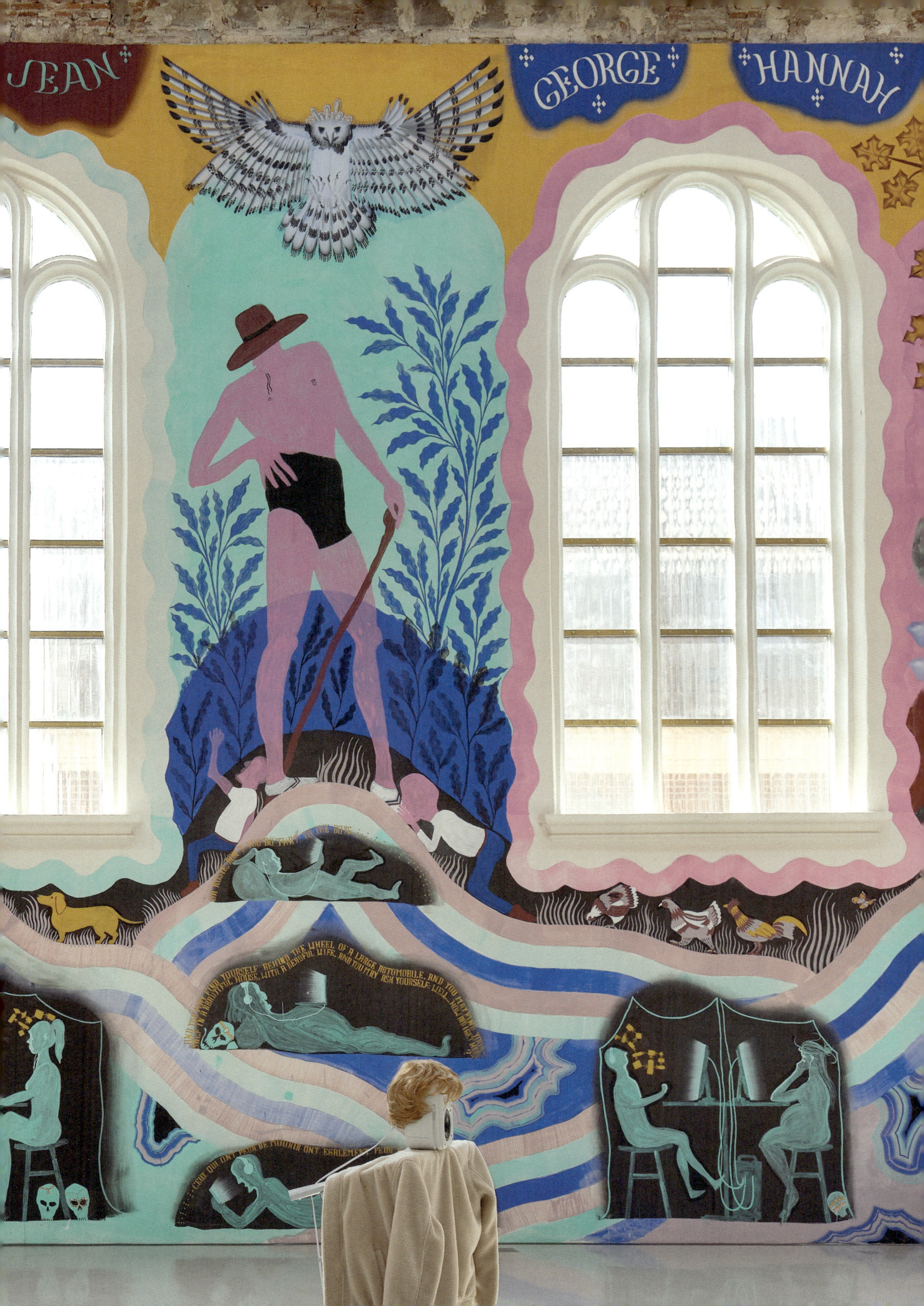
SEAN
GEORGE
HANNAH
AND YOU MAY FIND YOURSELF BEHIND THE WHEEL OF A LARGE AUTOMOBILE, AND YOU MAY FIND YOUR-
SELF IN A BEAUTIFUL HOUSE, WITH A BEAUFUL WIFE, AND YOU MAY ASK YOURSELF: WELL... HOW DID I GET HERE?
... CEUX QUI ONT PEUR DE MOURIR ONT EGALEMENT PEUR

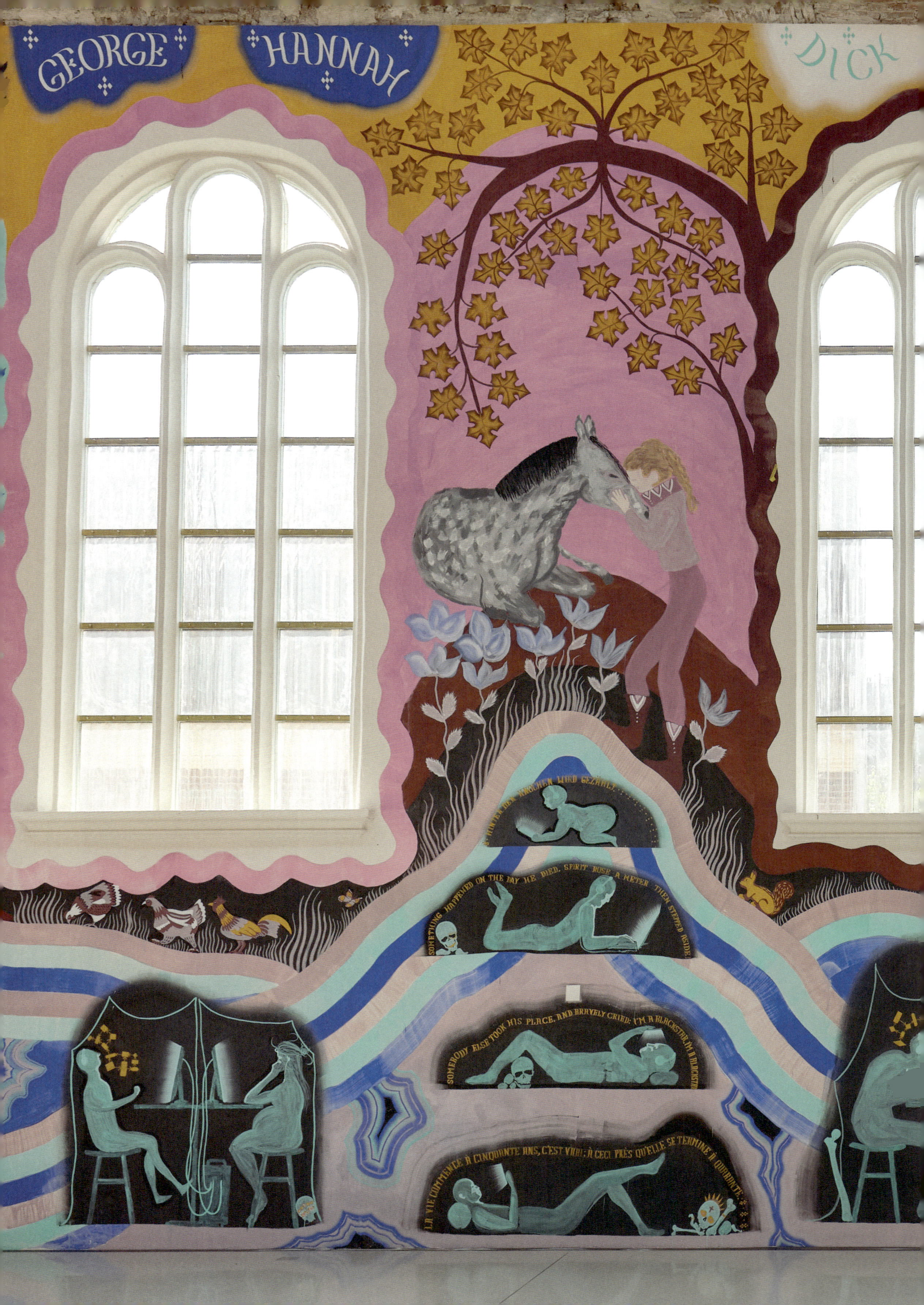
GEORGE
HANNAH
DICK
HINTER DEN KNOCHEN WIRD GEZÄHLT
SOMETHING HAPPENED ON THE DAY HE DIED, SPIRIT ROSE A METER THEN STEPPED ASIDE.
SOMEBODY ELSE TOOK HIS PLACE, AND BRAVELY CRIED: I'M A BLACKSTAR, I'M A
LA VIE COMMENCE À CINQUANTE ANS, C'EST VRAI; À CECI PRÈS QU'ELLE SE TERMINE À QUARANTE.

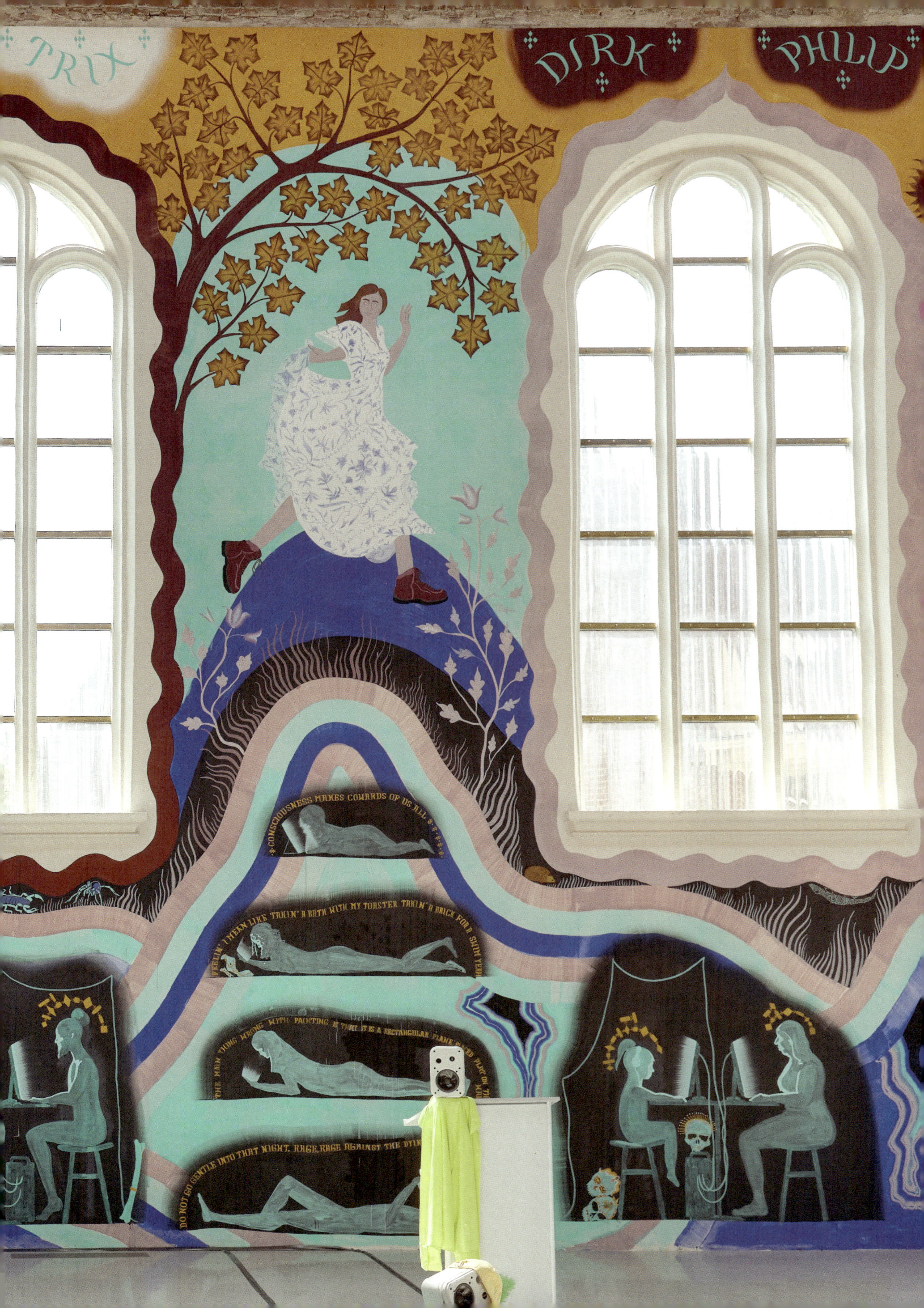
TRIX
DIRK
PHILIP
CONSCIOUSNESS MAKES COWARDS OF US ALL
FEELIN' I MEAN LIKE TAKIN' A BATH WITH MY TOASTER TAKIN' A BRICK FOR A SWIM YEAH
THE MAIN THING WRONG WITH PAINTING IS THAT IT IS A RECTANGULAR PLANE PLACED FLAT ON TH
DO NOT GO GENTLE INTO THAT NIGHT. RAGE, RAGE AGAINST THE DYIN

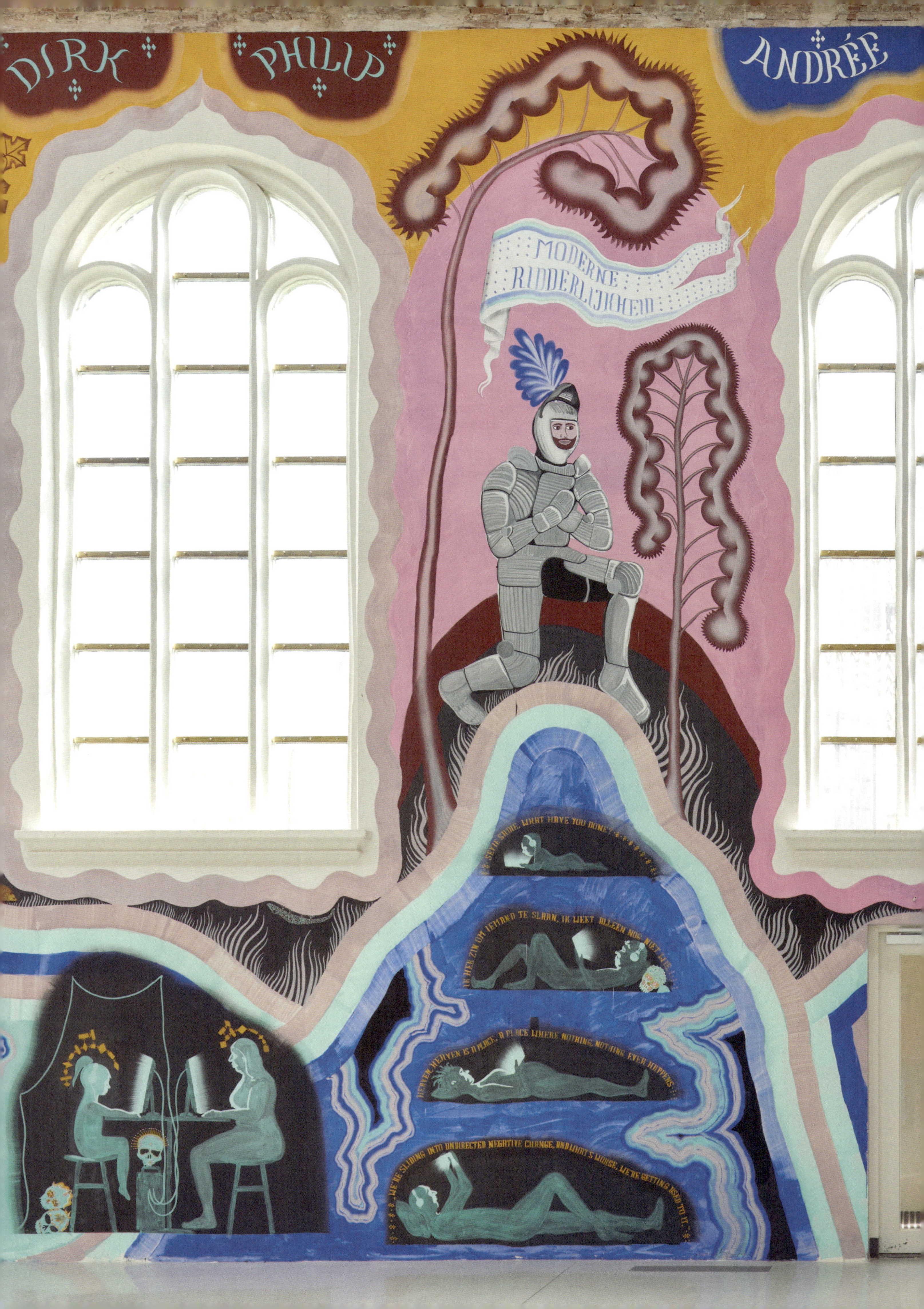
DIRK
PHILIP
ANDRÉE
MODERNE RIDDERLIJKHEID
SEXIE SADIE, WHAT HAVE YOU DONE?
IK HEB ZIN OM IEMAND TE SLAAN, IK WEET ALLEEN NOG NIET WIE
HEAVEN, HEAVEN IS A PLACE, A PLACE WHERE NOTHING, NOTHING EVER HAPPENS
WE'RE SLIDING INTO UNDIRECTED NEGATIVE CHANGE, AND WHAT'S WORSE, WE'RE GETTING USED TO IT.

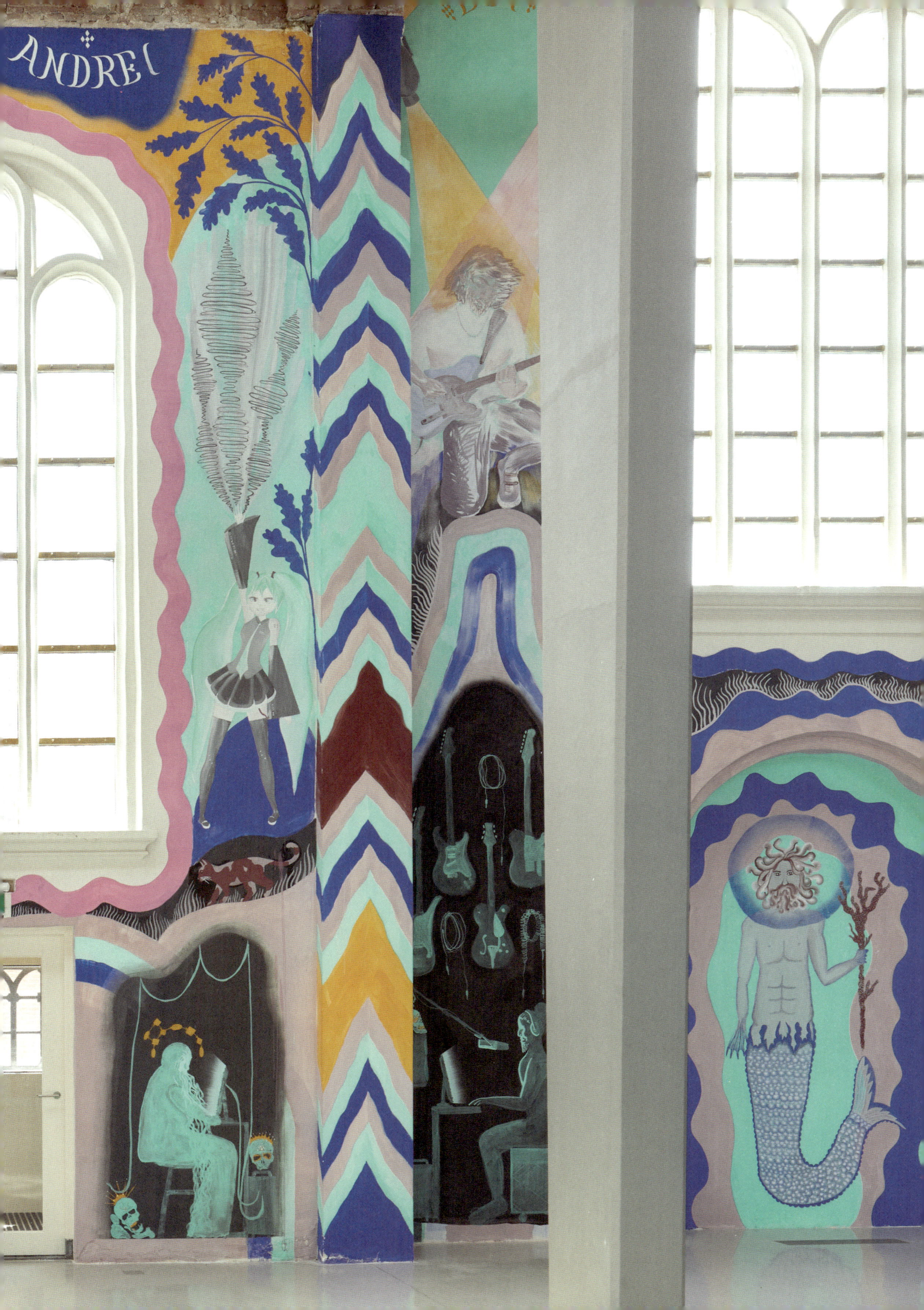
ANDREI

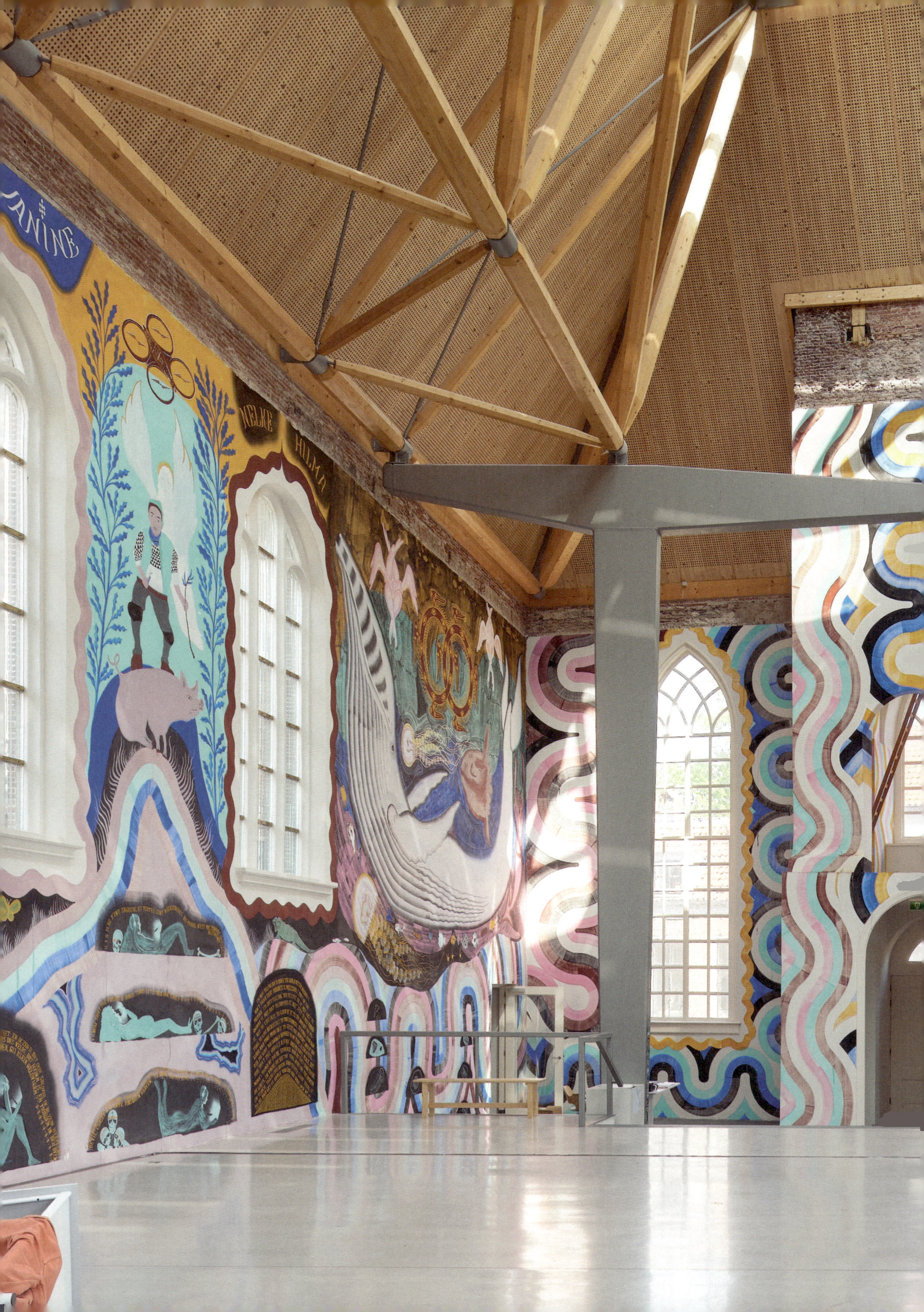
JANINE
NELKE
HILMA

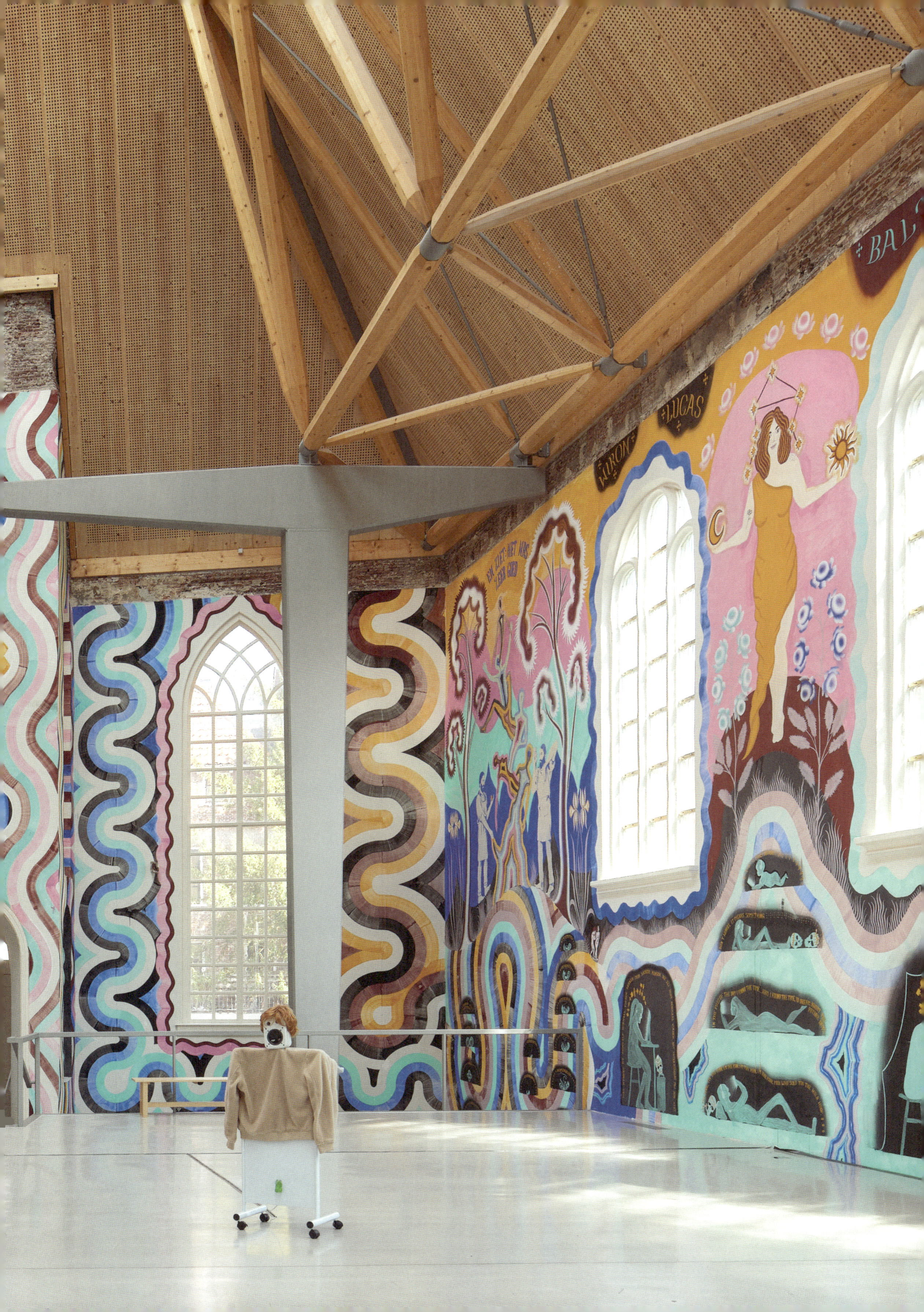

LUCAS

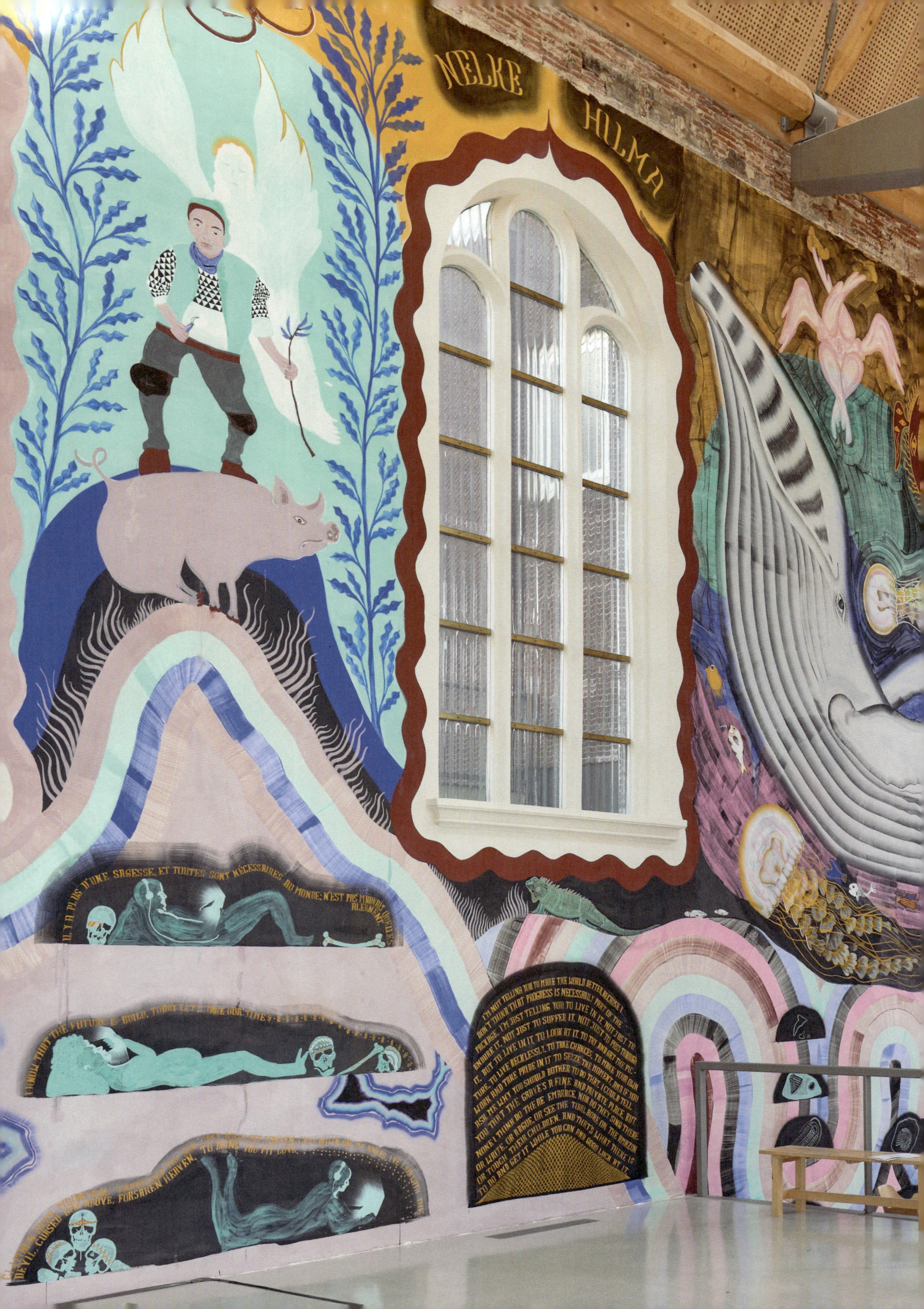
NELKE
HILMA
IL Y A PLUS D'UNE SAGESSE, ET TOUTES SONT NÉCESSAIRES AU MONDE; N'EST PAS MAUVAIS QU'ELLES ALERNENT.
I KNOW THAT THE FUTURE IS BUILD, TODAY LET'S TAKE OUR TIME
DEVIL. CURSED GOD ABOVE, FORSAKEN HEAVEN. TO BRING YOU MY LOVE.
I'M NOT TELLING YOU TO MAKE THE WORLD BETTER, BECAUSE I DON'T THINK THAT PROGRESS IS NECESSARILY PART OF THE PACKAGE. I'M JUST TELLING YOU TO LIVE IN IT. NOT JUST TO ENDURE IT. NOT JUST TO SUFFER IT. NOT JUST TO PASS THROUGH IT. BUT TO LIVE IN IT, TO LOOK AT IT. TO TRY AND GET THE PICTURE. TO LIVE RECKLESSLY. TO TAKE CHANCES. TO MAKE YOUR OWN WORK AND TAKE PRIDE IN IT TO SEIZE THE MOMENT. AND IF YOU ASK ME WHY YOU SHOULD BOTHER TO DO THAT, I COULD TELL YOU THAT THE GRAVE'S A FINE AND PRIVATE PLACE, BUT NONE I THINK DO THERE EMBRACE. NOR DO THEY SING THERE. OR WRITE, OR ARGUE, OR SEE THE TIDAL BORE ON THE AMAZON OR TOUCH THEIR CHILDREN. AND THAT'S WHAT THERE IS TO DO AND GET IT WHILE YOU CAN AND GOOD LUCK AT IT.

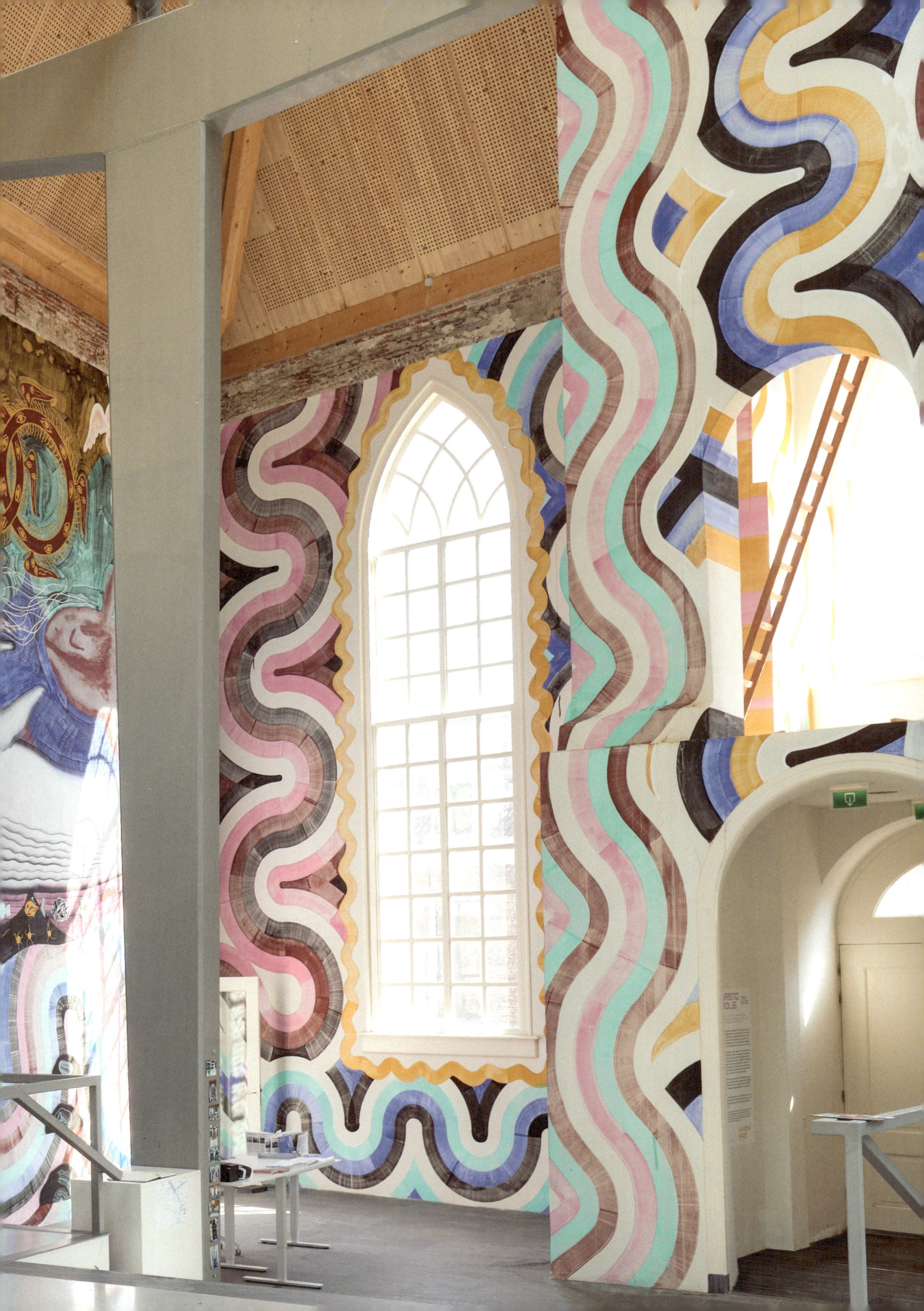

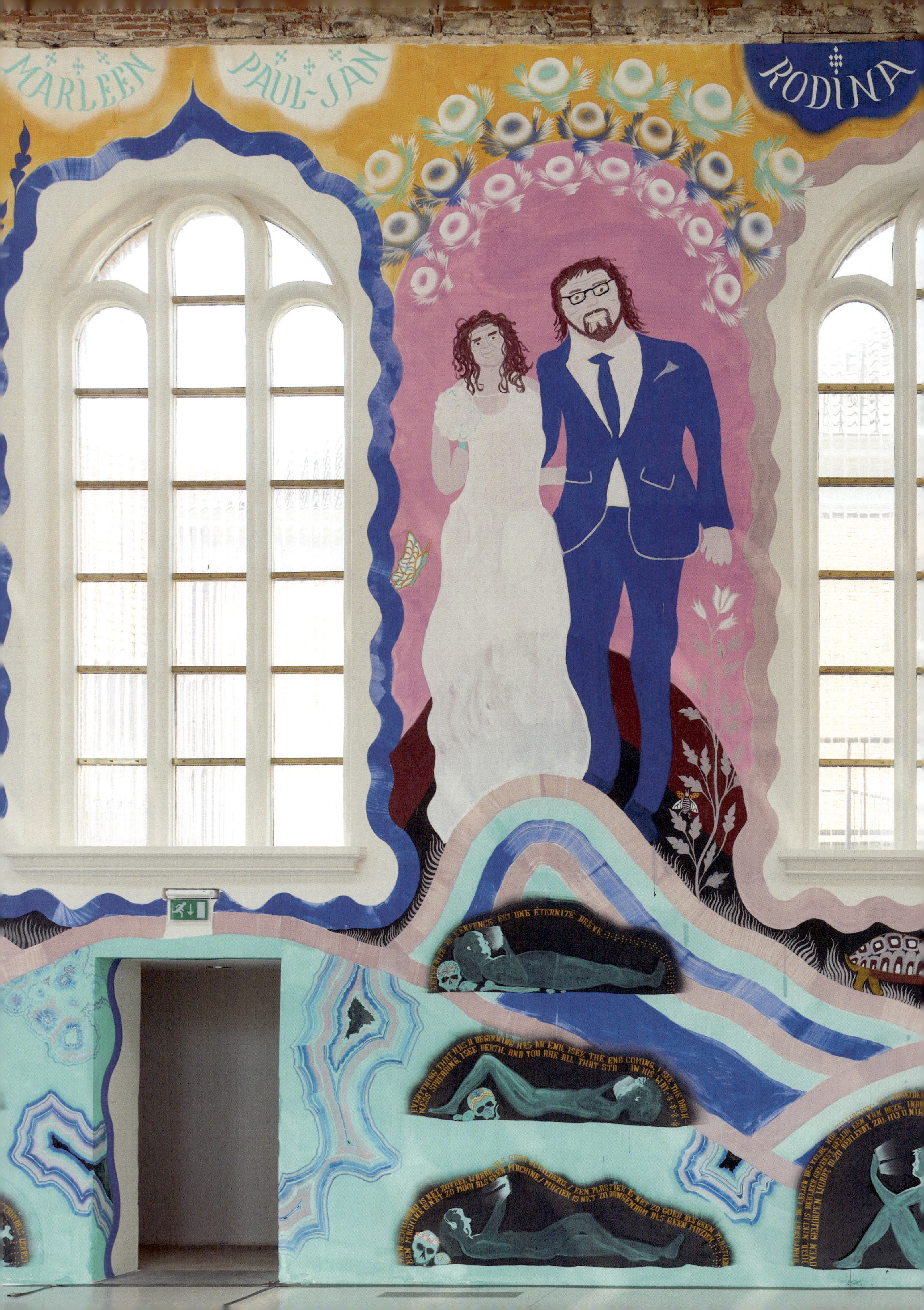
MARLEEN
PAUL-JAN
RODINA
ÉTERNITÉ DE L'ENFANCE EST UNE ÉTERNITÉ BRÈVE
EVERYTHING THAT HAS A BEGINNING HAS AN END. I SEE THE END COMING. I SEE THE DARK-
NESS SPREADING. I SEE DEATH. AND YOU ARE ALL THAT STA IN HIS WAY.
EEN SCHILDERIJ IS NET ZOVEEL WAARD ALS GEEN SCHILDERIJ / EEN PLASTIEK IS NET ZO GOED ALS GEEN PLASTIEK
EEN MACHINE IS NET ZO MOOI ALS GEEN MACHINE / MUZIEK IS NET ZO AANGENAAM ALS GEEN MUZIEK

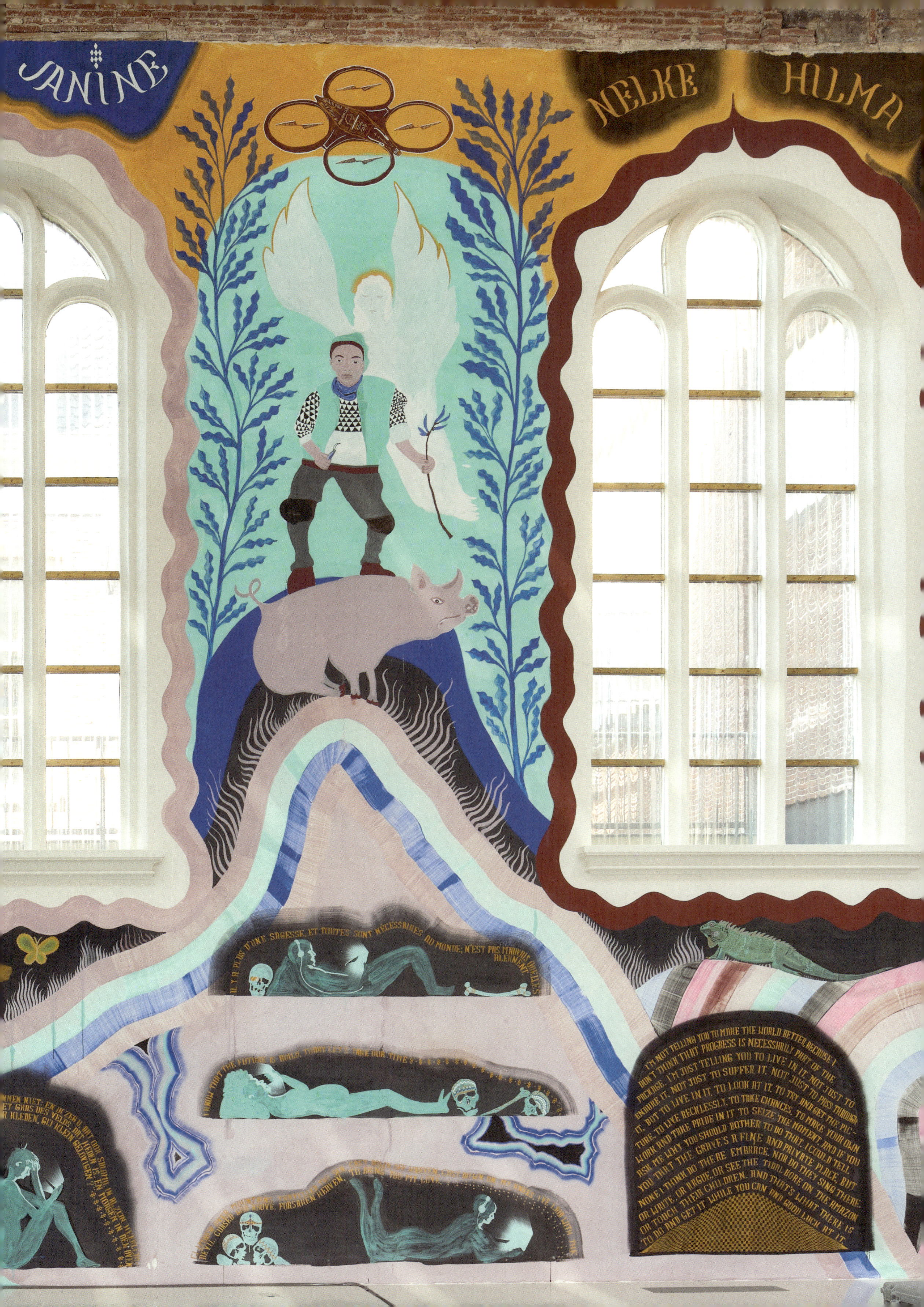
JANINE
NELKE
HILMA
IL Y A PLUS D'UNE SAGESSE, ET TOUTES SONT NÉCESSAIRES AU MONDE; N'EST PAS MAUVAIS QU'ELLES ALTERNENT
I'M NOT TELLING YOU TO MAKE THE WORLD BETTER, BECAUSE I DON'T THINK THAT PROGRESS IS NECESSARILY PART OF THE PACKAGE. I'M JUST TELLING YOU TO LIVE IN IT. NOT JUST TO ENDURE IT. NOT JUST TO SUFFER IT. NOT JUST TO PASS THROUGH IT. BUT TO LIVE IN IT. TO LOOK AT IT. TO TRY AND GET THE PICTURE. TO LIVE RECKLESSLY. TO TAKE CHANCES. TO MAKE YOUR OWN WORK AND TAKE PRIDE IN IT. TO SEIZE THE MOMENT. AND IF YOU ASK ME WHY YOU SHOULD BOTHER TO DO THAT, I COULD TELL YOU THAT THE GRAVE'S A FINE AND PRIVATE PLACE, BUT NONE I THINK DO THERE EMBRACE. NOR DO THEY SING THERE, OR WRITE, OR ARGUE, OR SEE THE TIDAL BORE ON THE AMAZON OR TOUCH THEIR CHILDREN. AND THAT'S WHAT THERE IS TO DO AND GET IT WHILE YOU CAN AND GOOD LUCK AT IT.

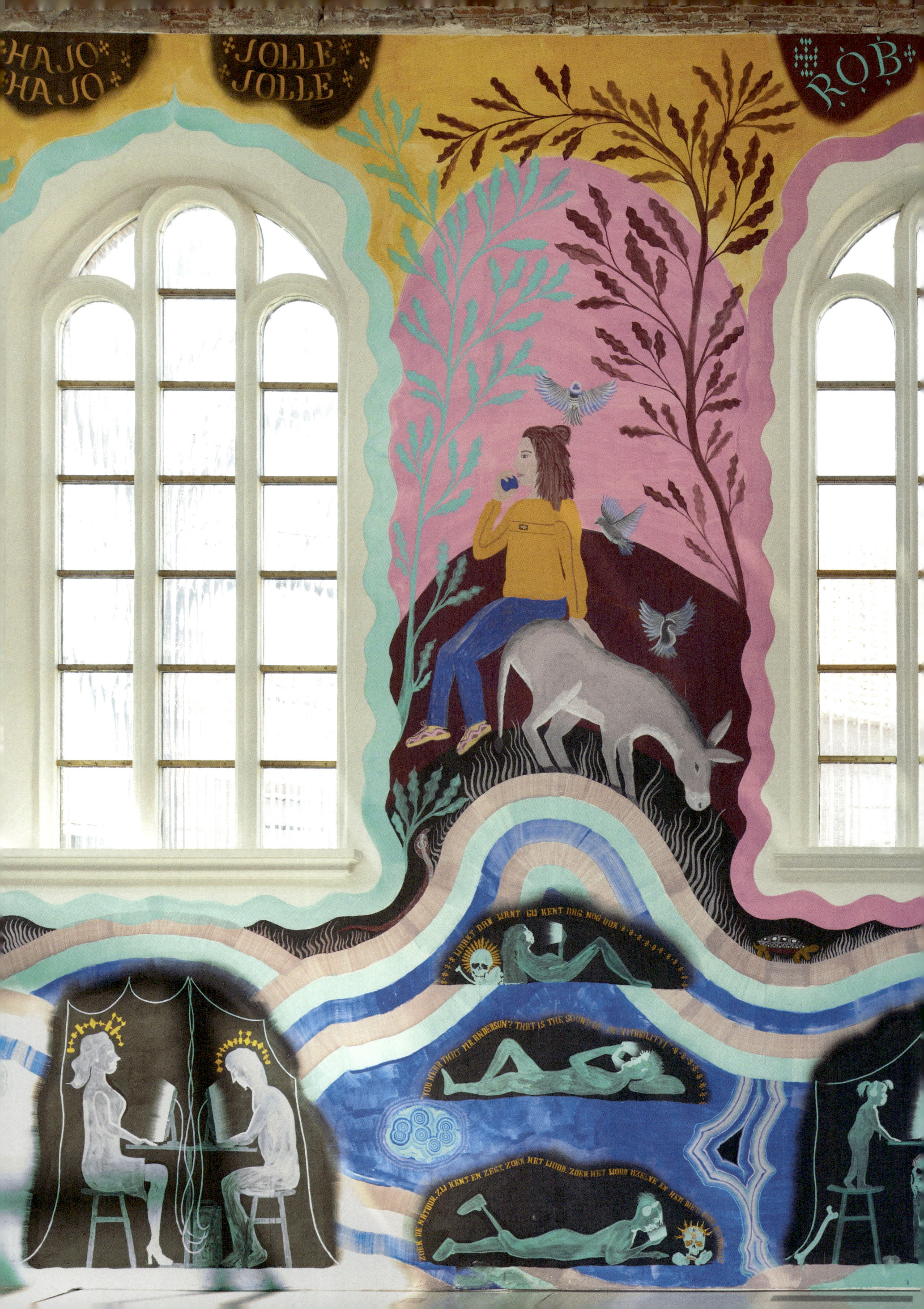
HAJO
HAJO
JOLLE
JOLLE
ROB
WAAKT DAN WANT GIJ KENT DAG NOG UUR
YOU HEAR THAT MR.ANDERSON? THAT IS THE SOUND OF INEVITABILITY!
ZOEK DE NATUUR. ZIJ KENT EN ZEGT. ZOEK HET WOUD. ZOEK HET WOUD UZELVE EN HEM DIE

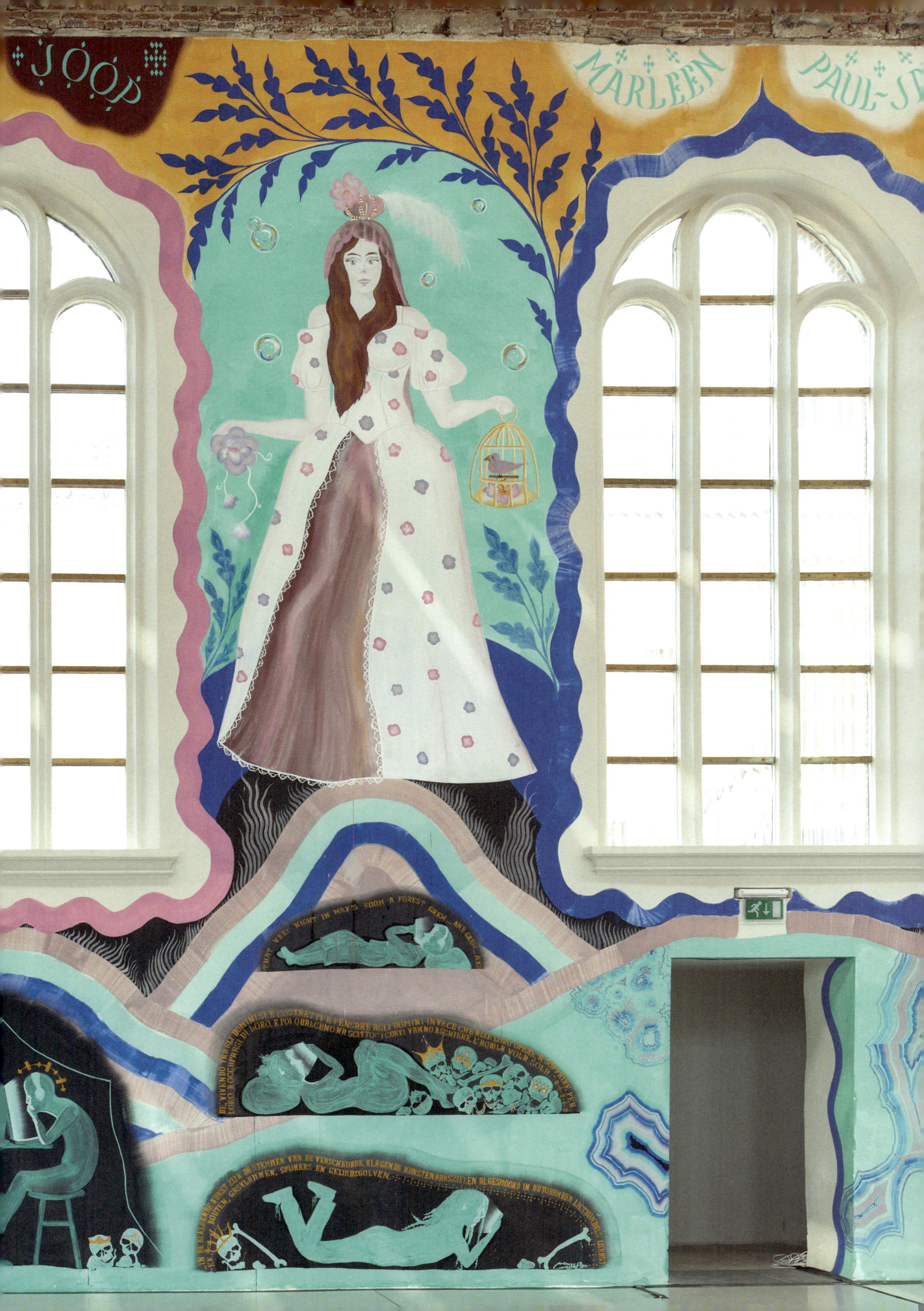
JOOP
MARLEEN
THAT VERY NIGHT IN MAX'S ROOM A FOREST GREW... AND GREW...
BE' VIVENDO TRA GLI UOMINI SI È COSTRETTI A PENSARE AGLI UOMINI INVECE CHE ALLE LORO OPERE, A SCRIVERE PER LORO, A OCCUPARSI DI LORO, E POI QUALCUNO HA SCITTO: "I CORVI VANNO A SCHIERE, L'AQUILA VOLA SOLA"
IN DE BEELDENDE KUNST ZIJN DE STEMMEN VAN DE VERSCHEURDE, KLAGENDE KUNSTENAARSZIELEN AL GESMOORD IN AUTOBANDEN
GASVLAMMEN, SPOKERS EN GELUIDSGOLVEN.

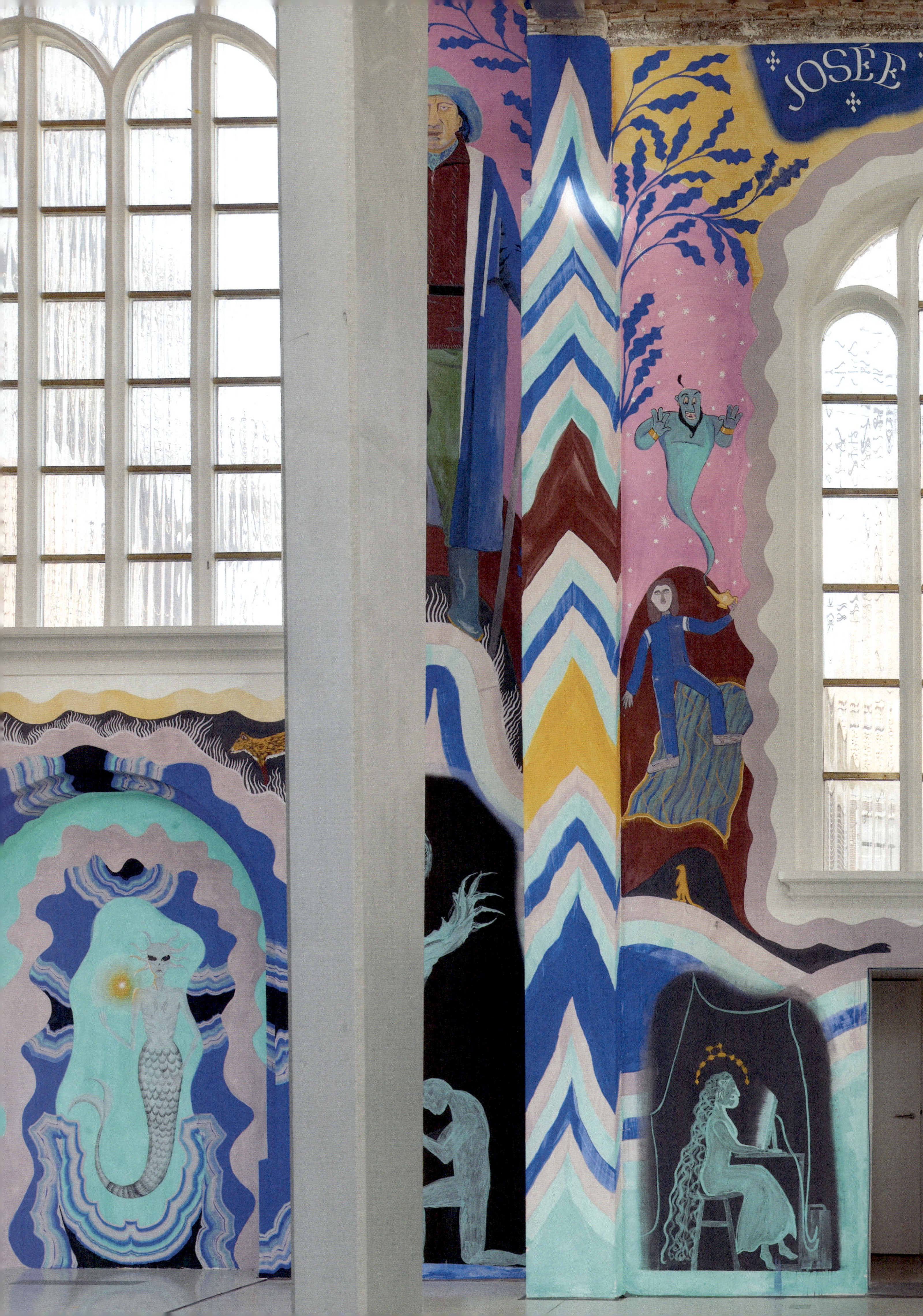
JOSÉE

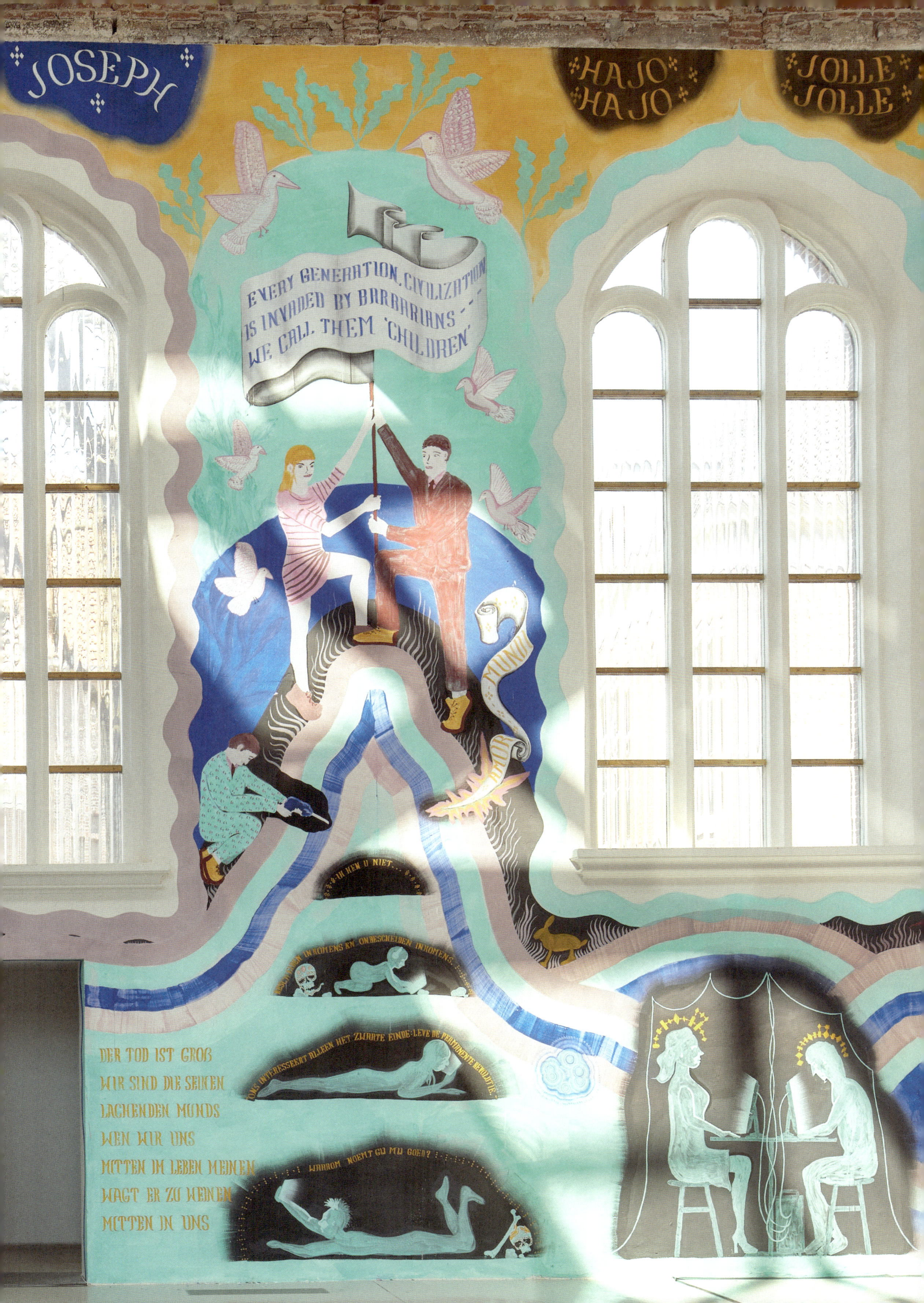
JOSEPH
HAJO
HAJO
JOLLE
JOLLE
EVERY GENERATION, CIVILIZATION
IS INVADED BY BARBARIANS - - -
WE CALL THEM 'CHILDREN'
UI KEN U NIET...
BESCHEIDEN INKOMENS EN ONBESCHEIDEN INKOMENS.
ONS INTERESSEERT ALLEEN HET ZWARTE EINDE: LEVE DE PERMANENTE REVOLUTIE.
WAAROM NOEMT GIJ MIJ GOED?
DER TOD IST GROß
WIR SIND DIE SEINEN
LACHENDEN MUNDS
WEN WIR UNS
MITTEN IM LEBEN MEINEN
WAGT ER ZU WEINEN
MITTEN IN UNS

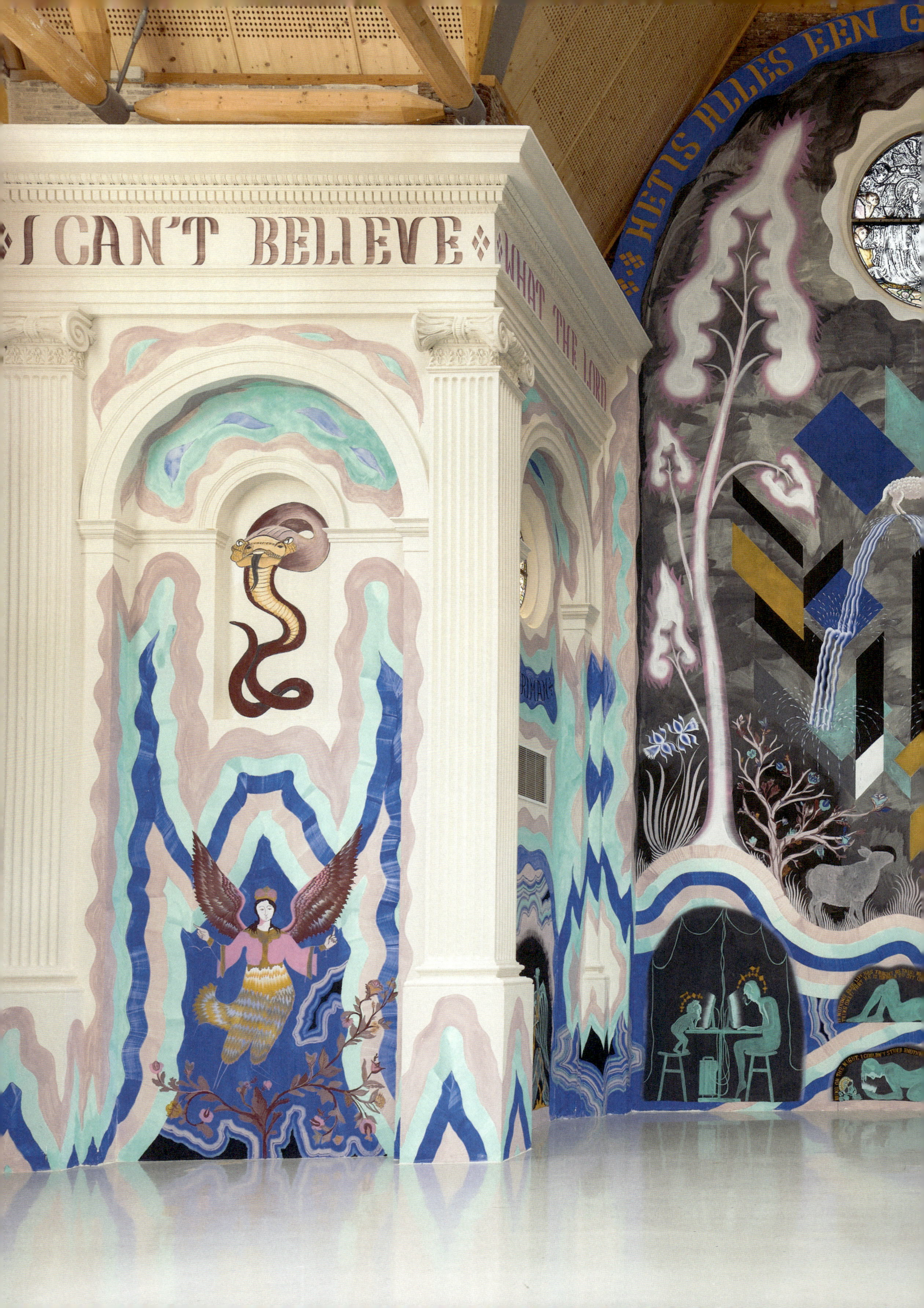
I CAN'T BELIEVE
WHAT THE LORD
HET IS ALLES EEN

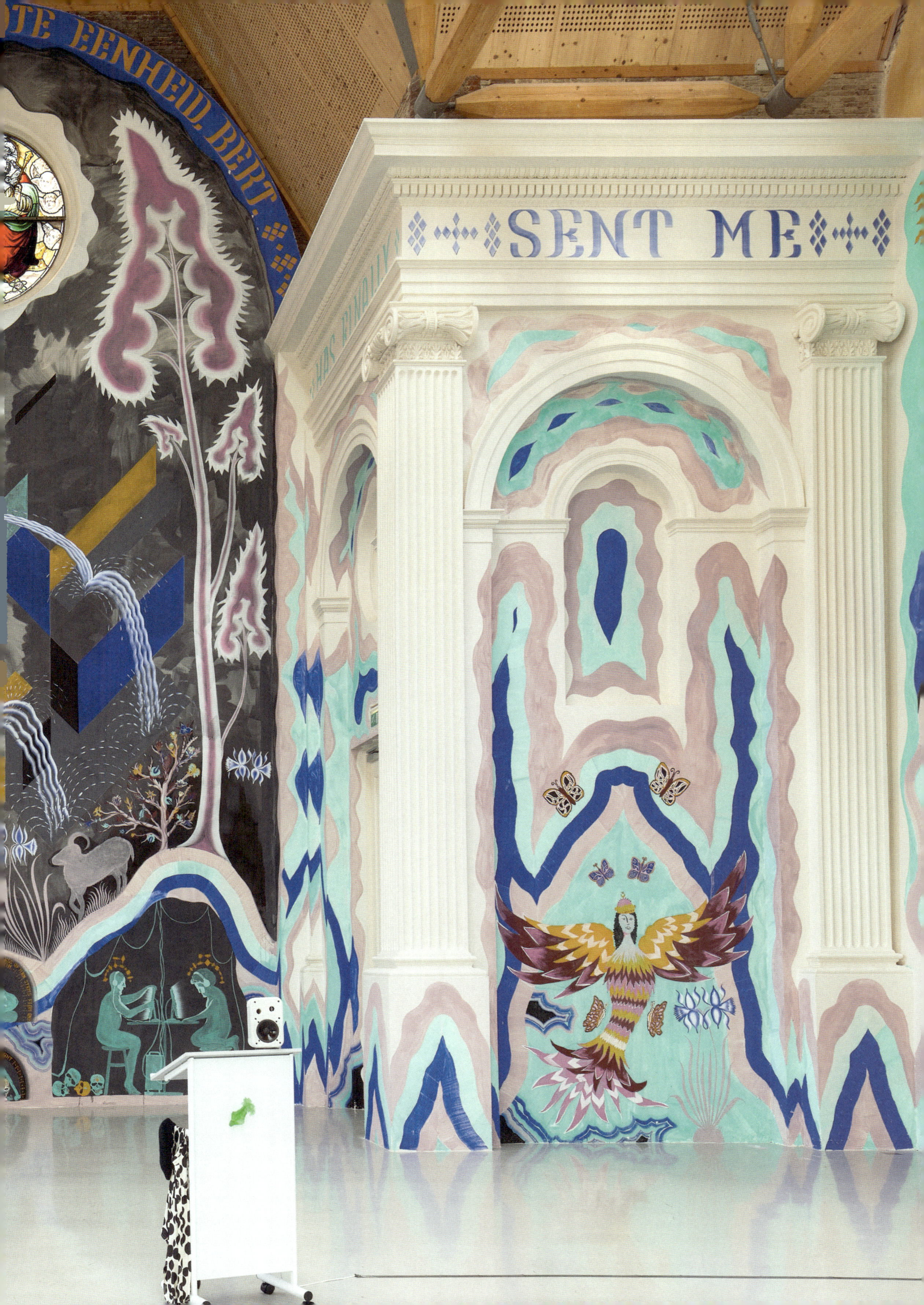
TE EENHEID. BERT.
SENT ME

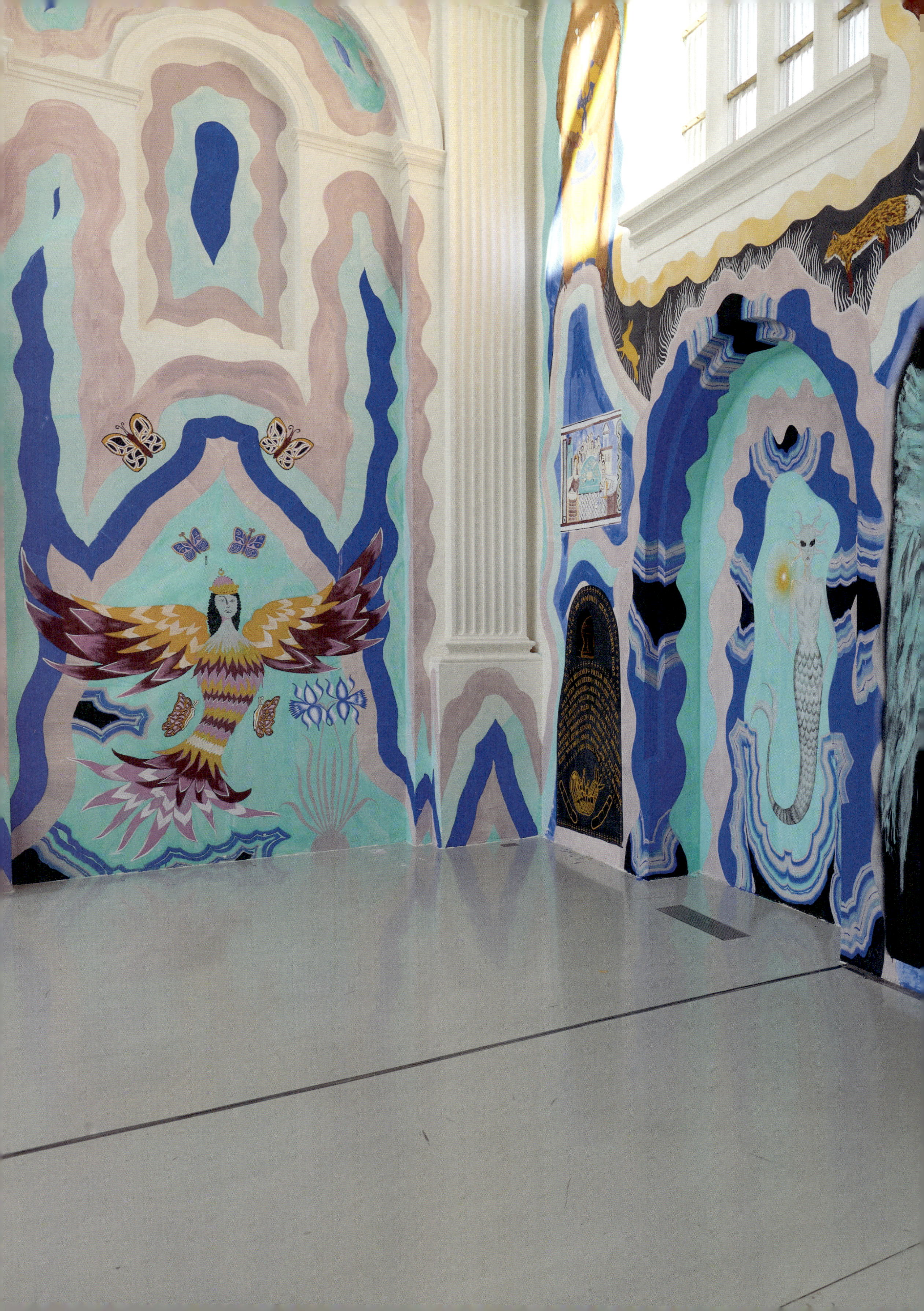

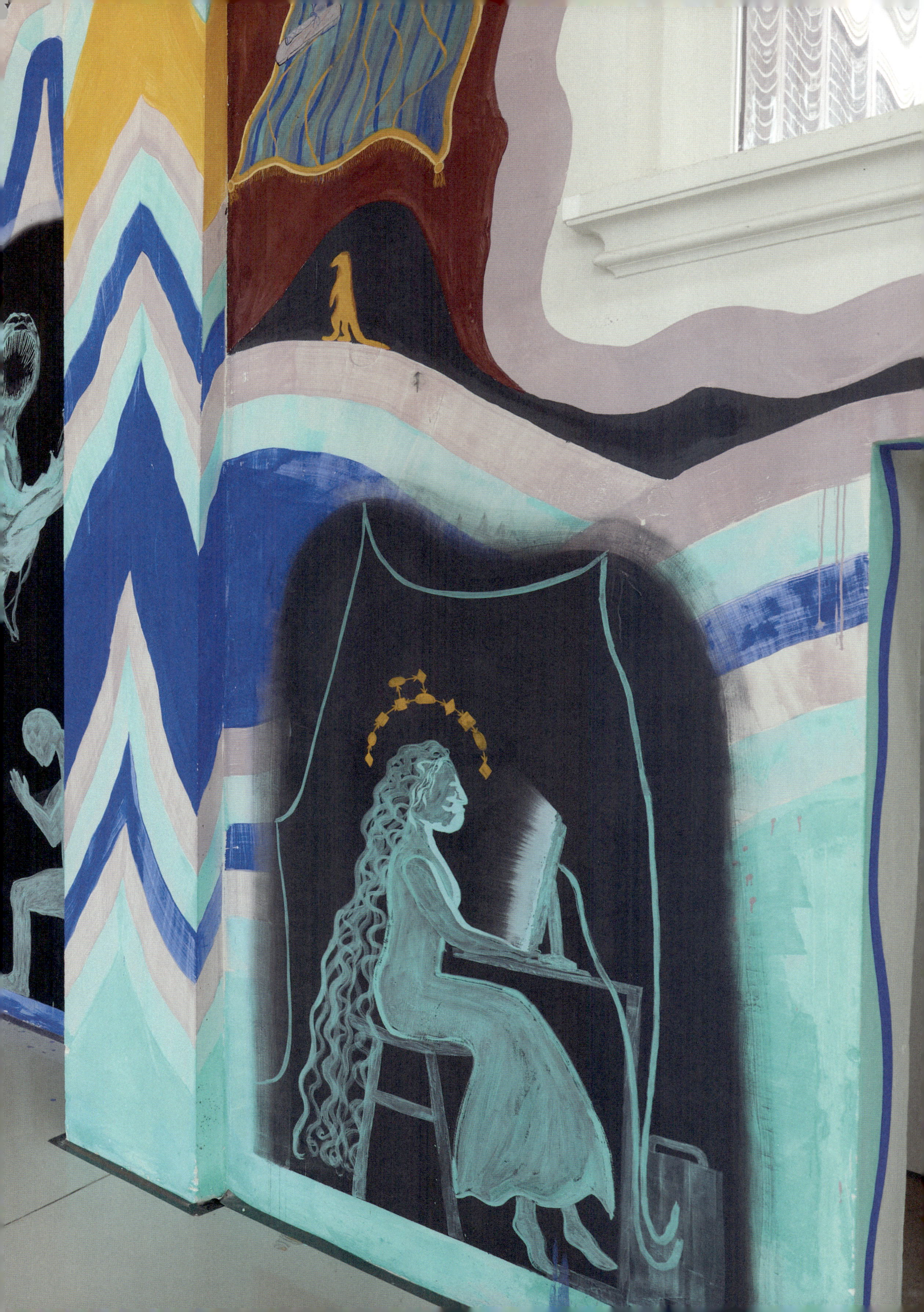

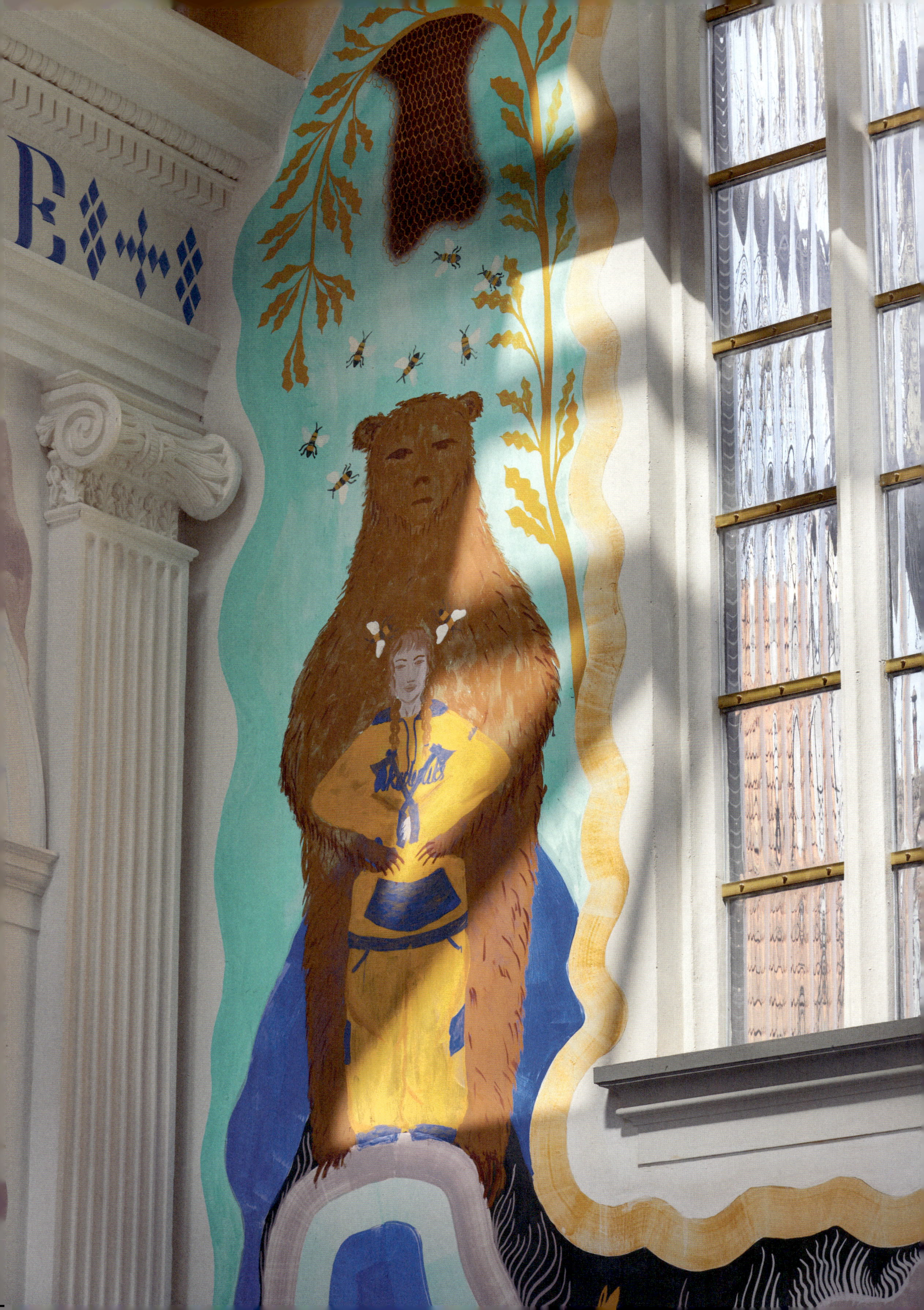

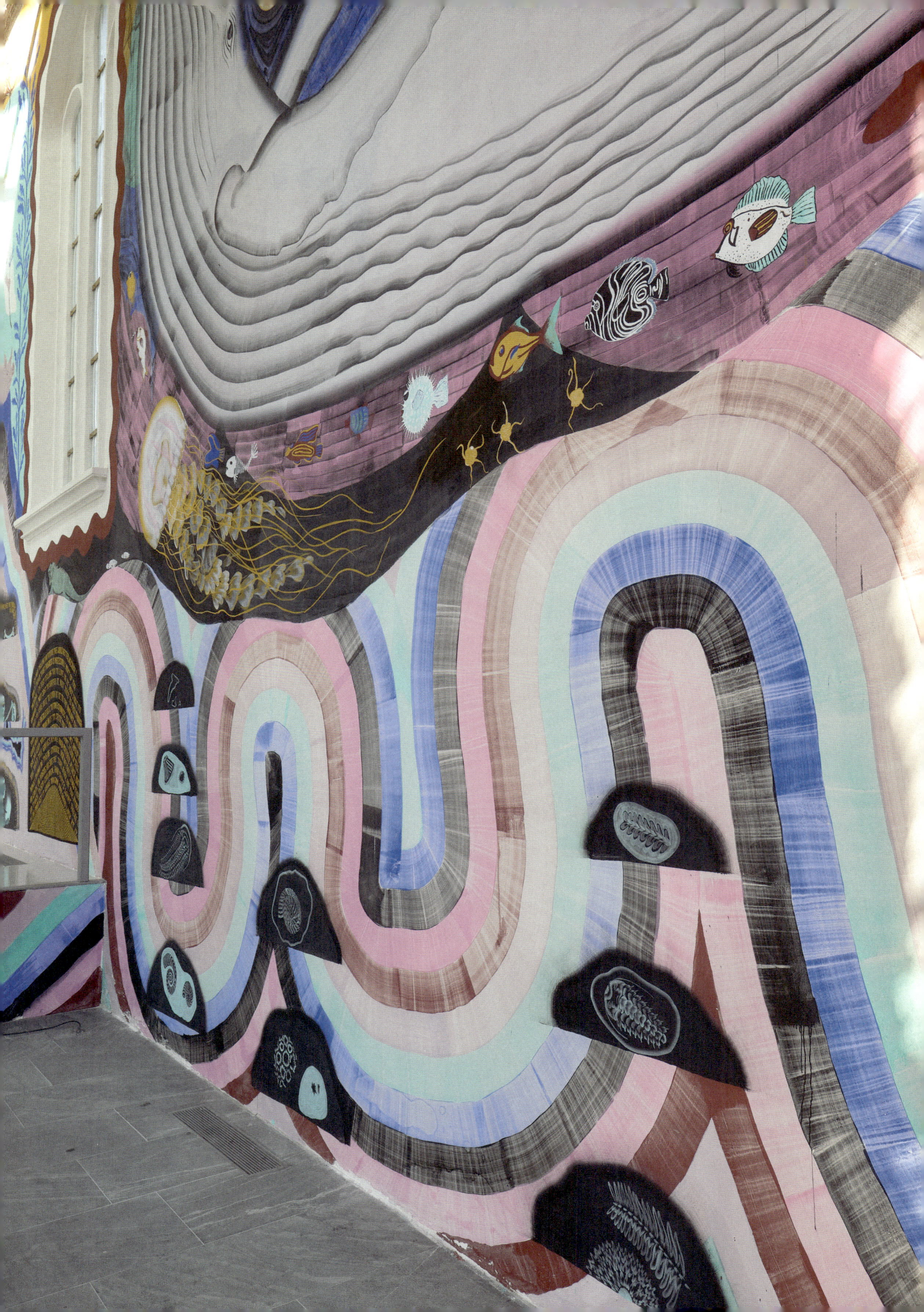

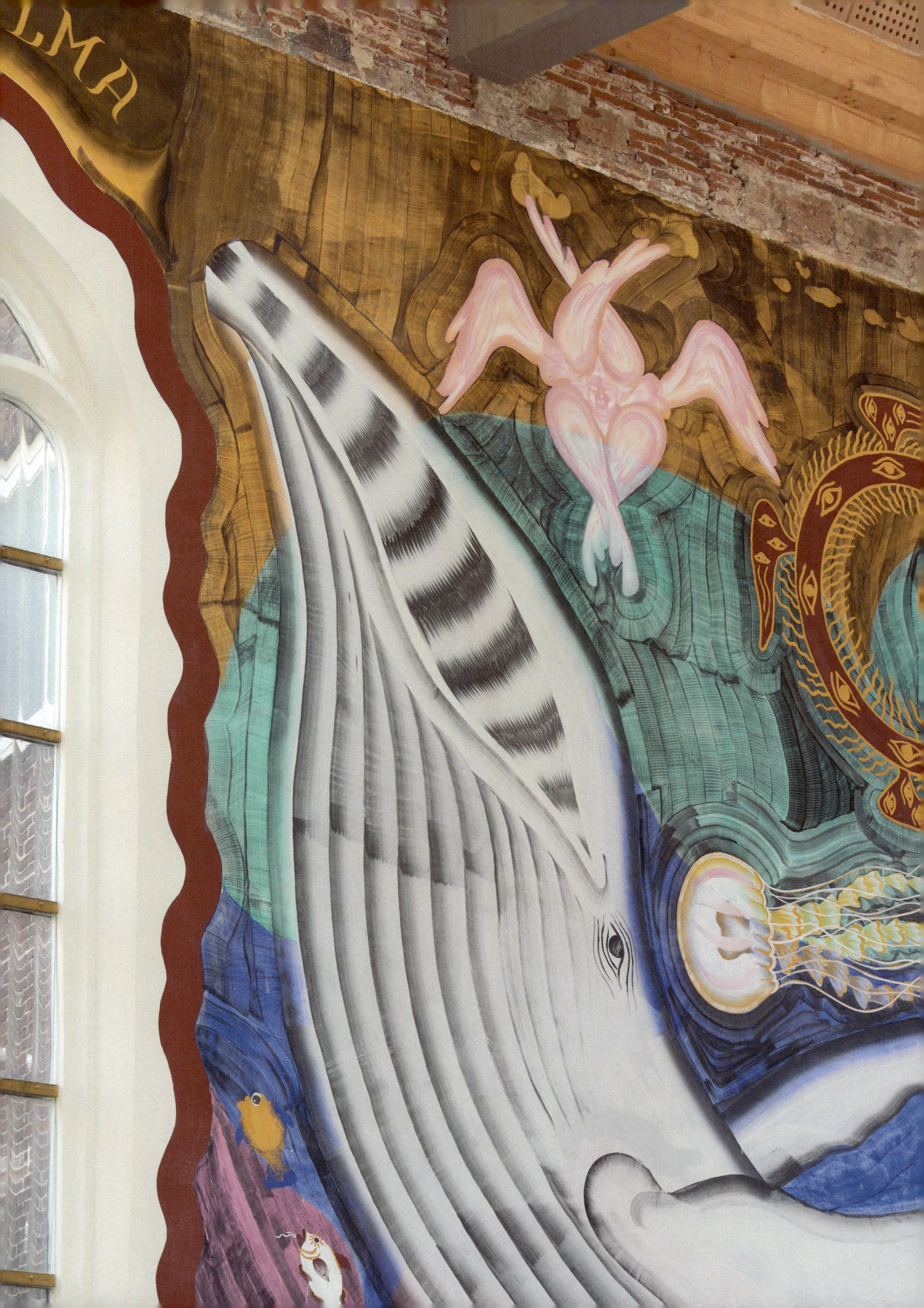
LMA

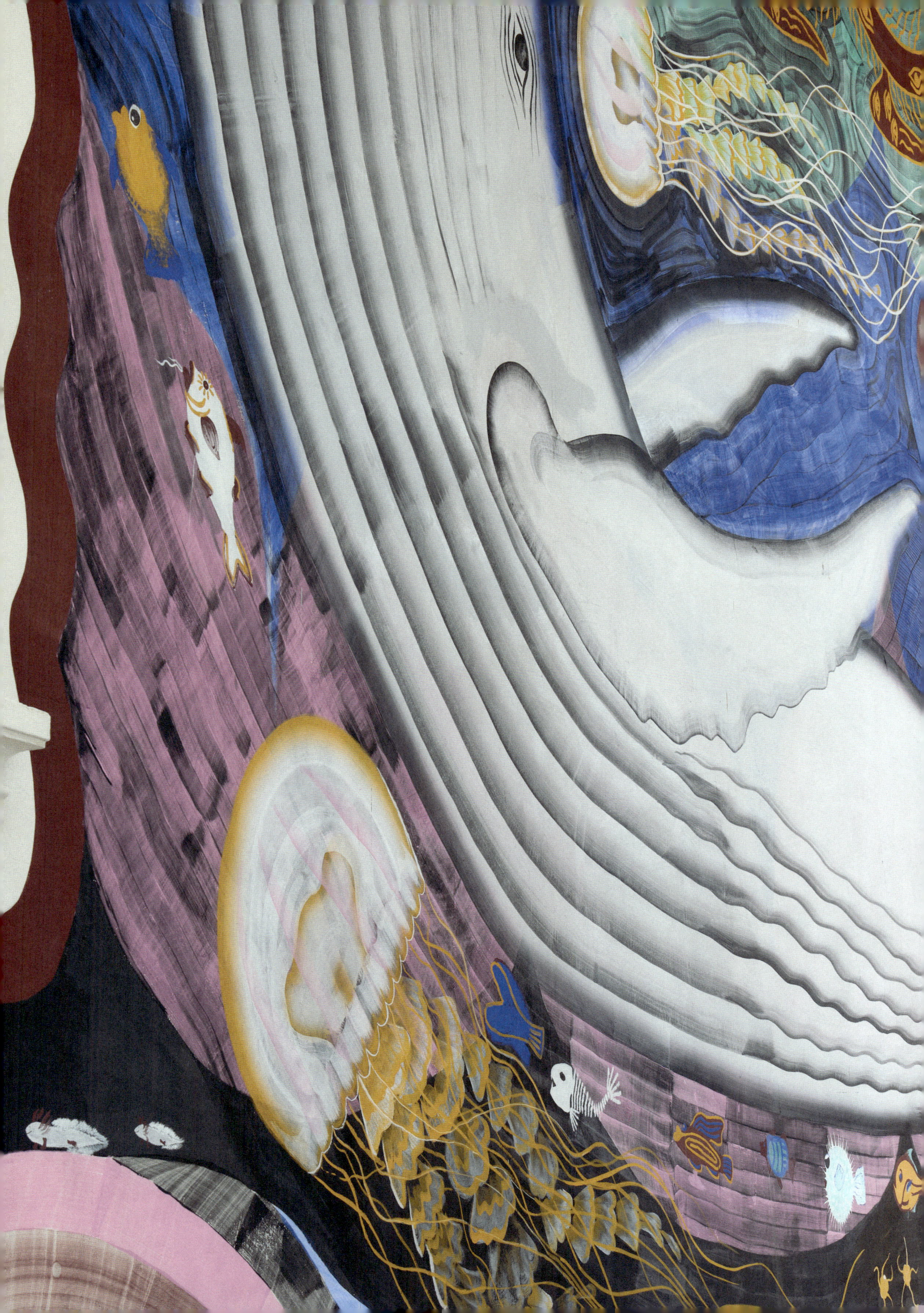

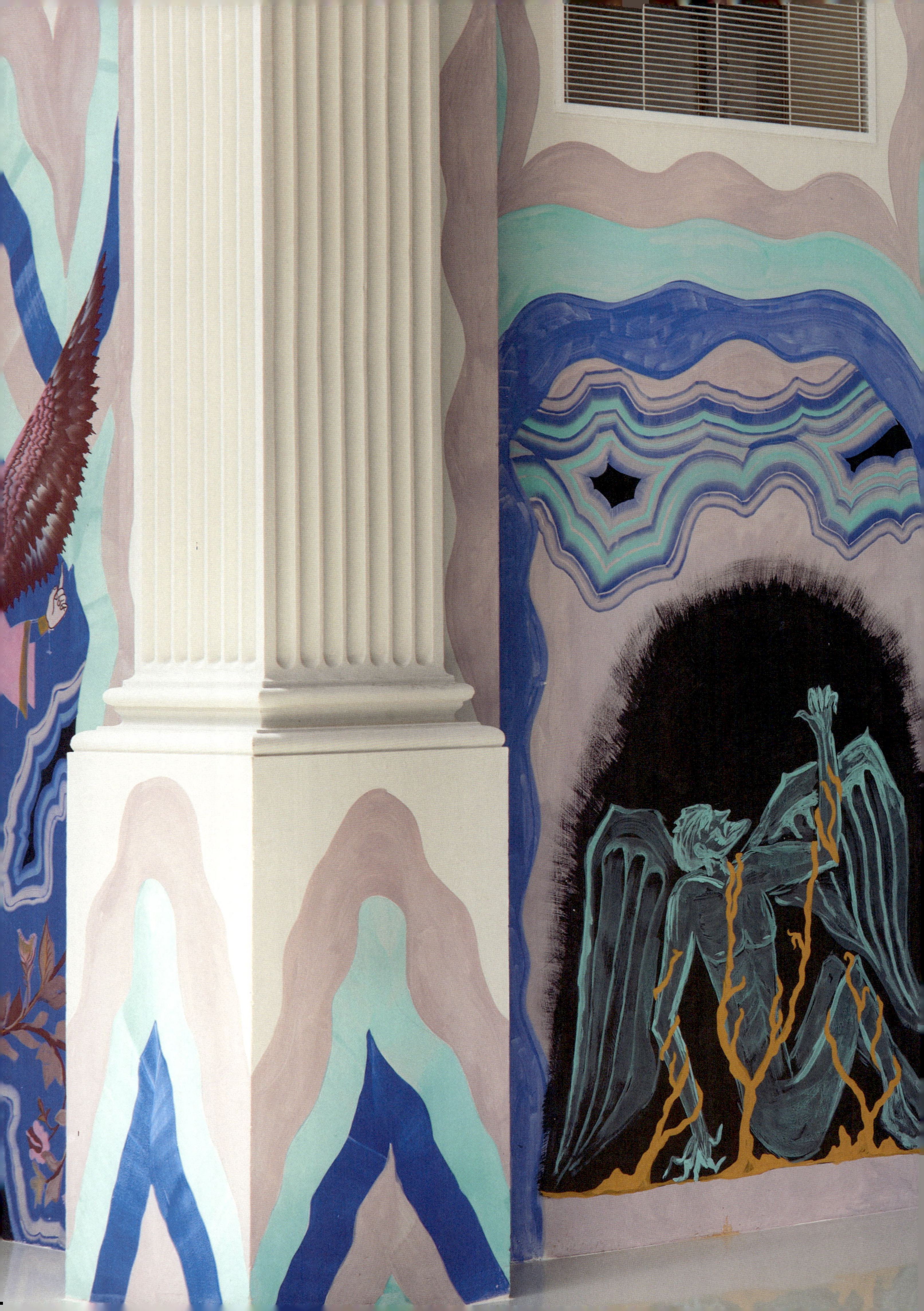

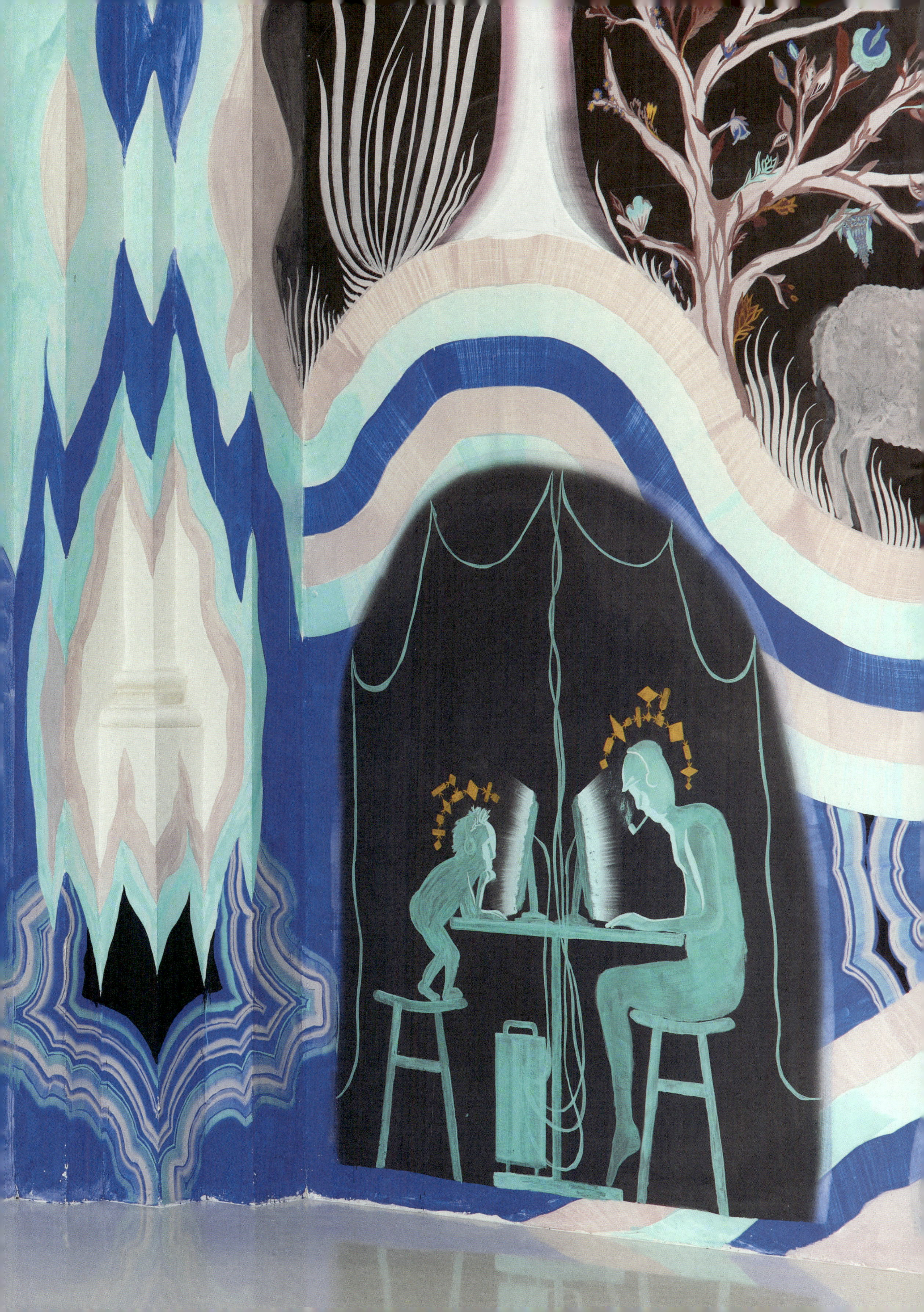

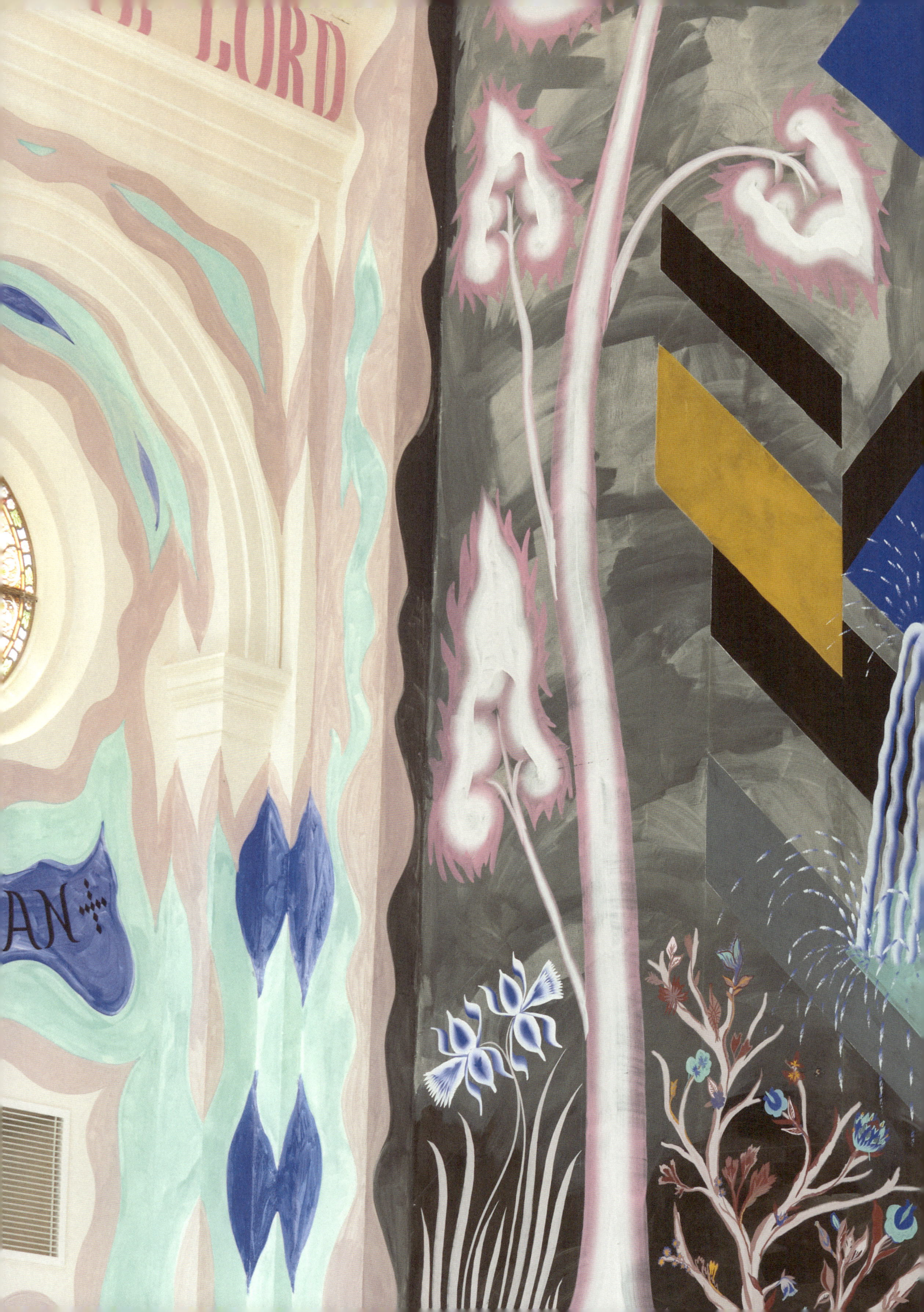
LORD

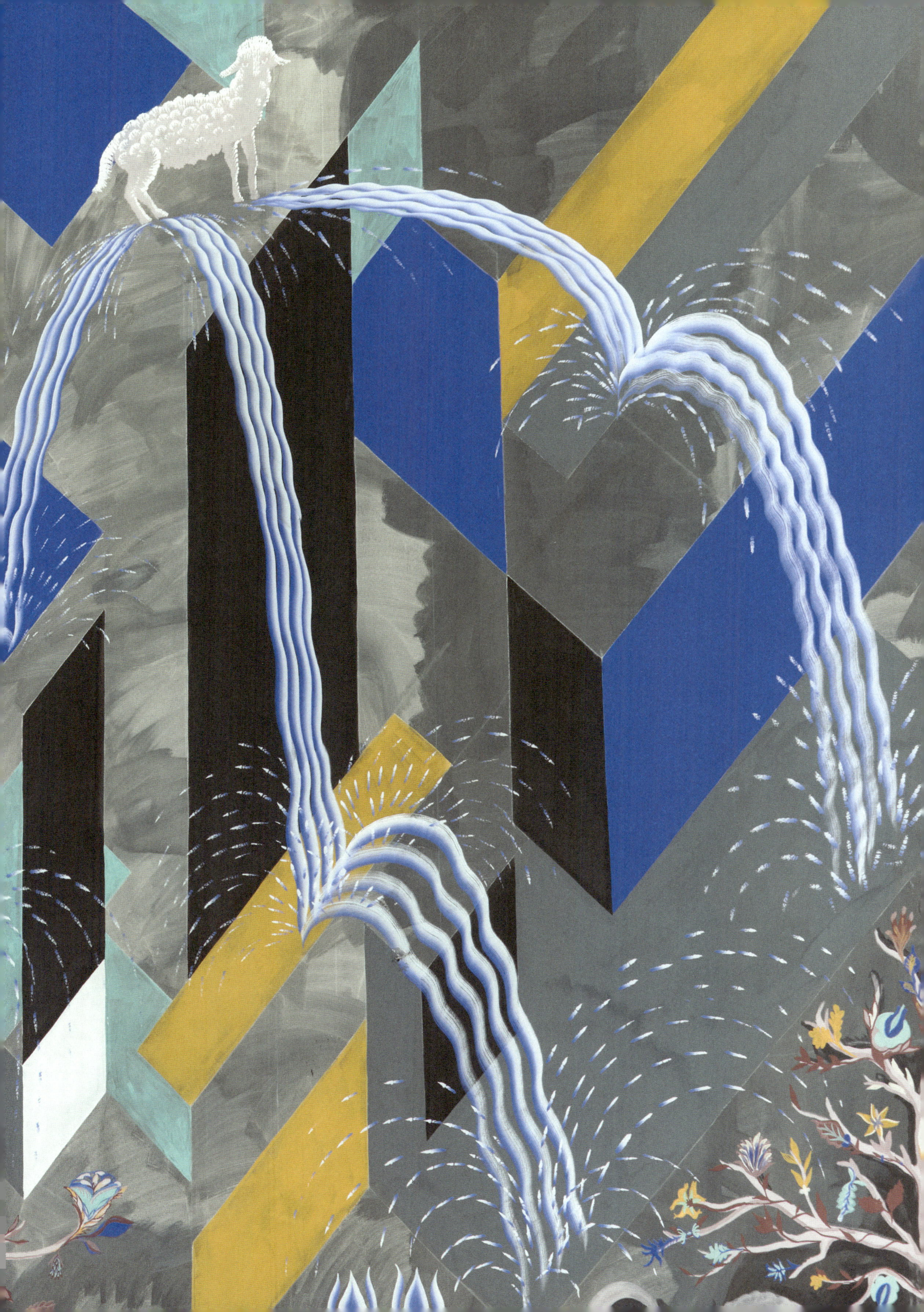

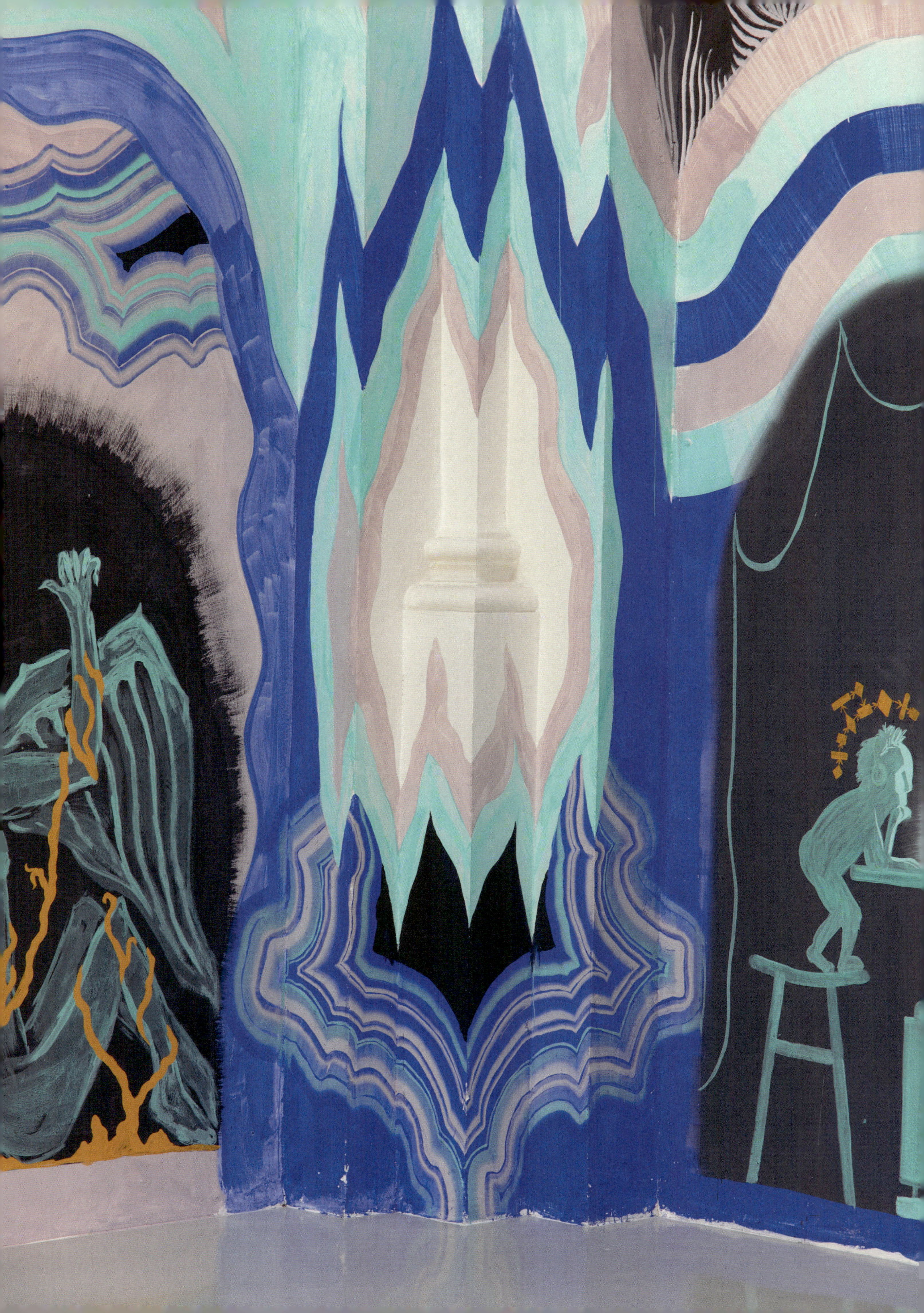

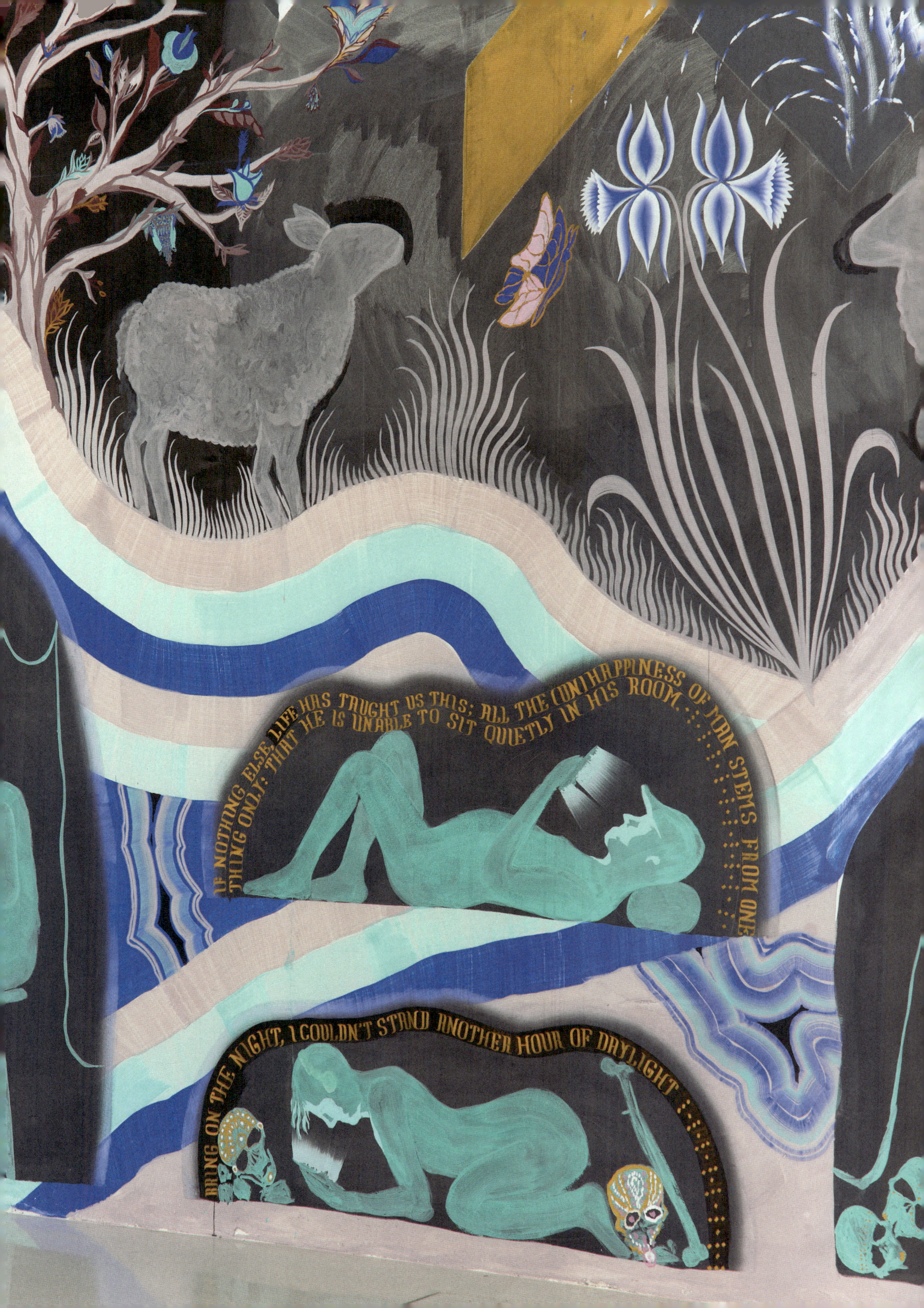

IF NOTHING ELSE, LIFE HAS TAUGHT US THIS; ALL THE (UN)HAPPINESS OF MAN STEMS FROM ONE
THING ONLY: THAT HE IS UNABLE TO SIT QUIETLY IN HIS ROOM
BRING ON THE NIGHT, I COULDN'T STAND ANOTHER HOUR OF DAYLIGHT

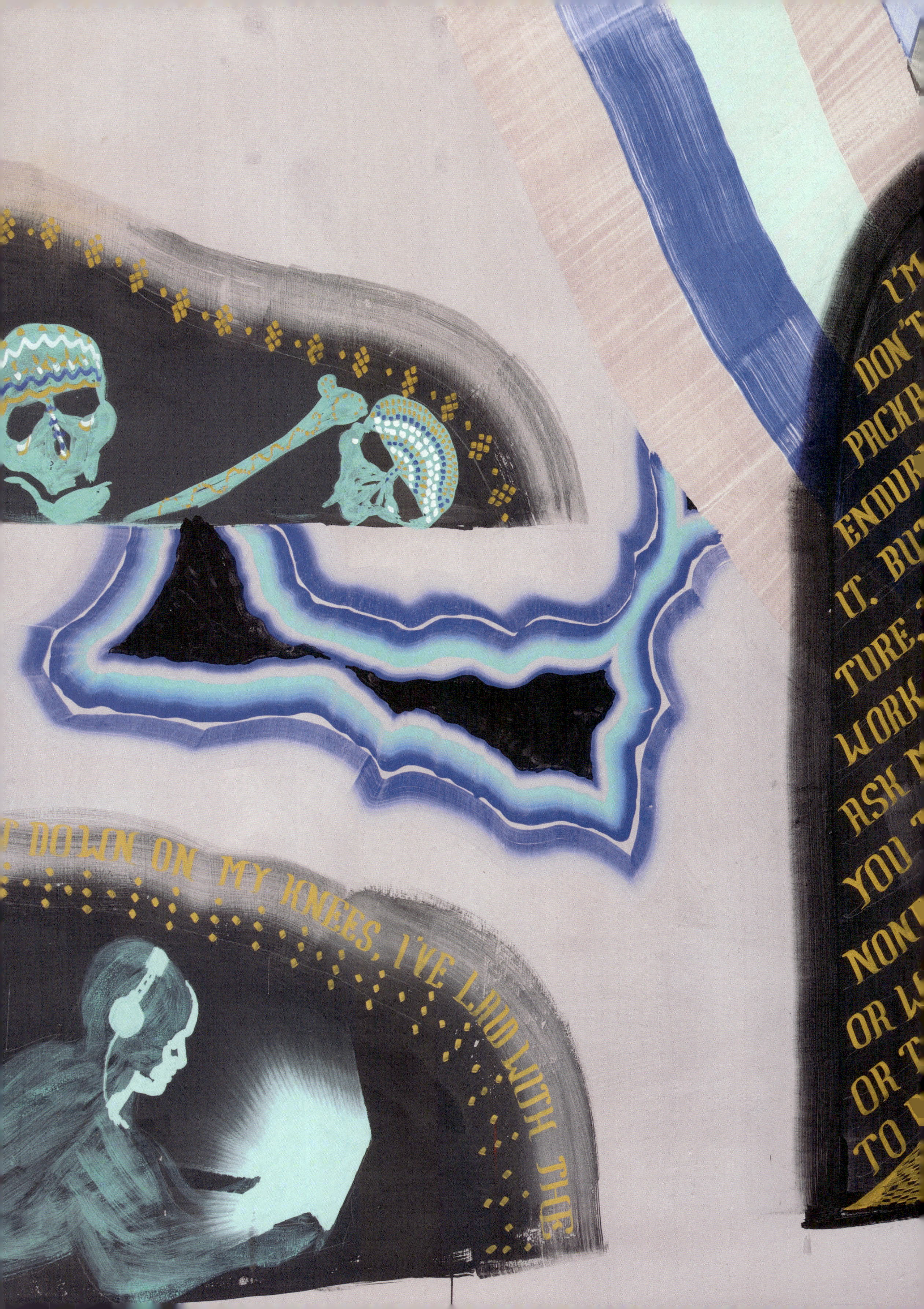
DOWN ON MY KNEES, I'VE LAID WITH THE

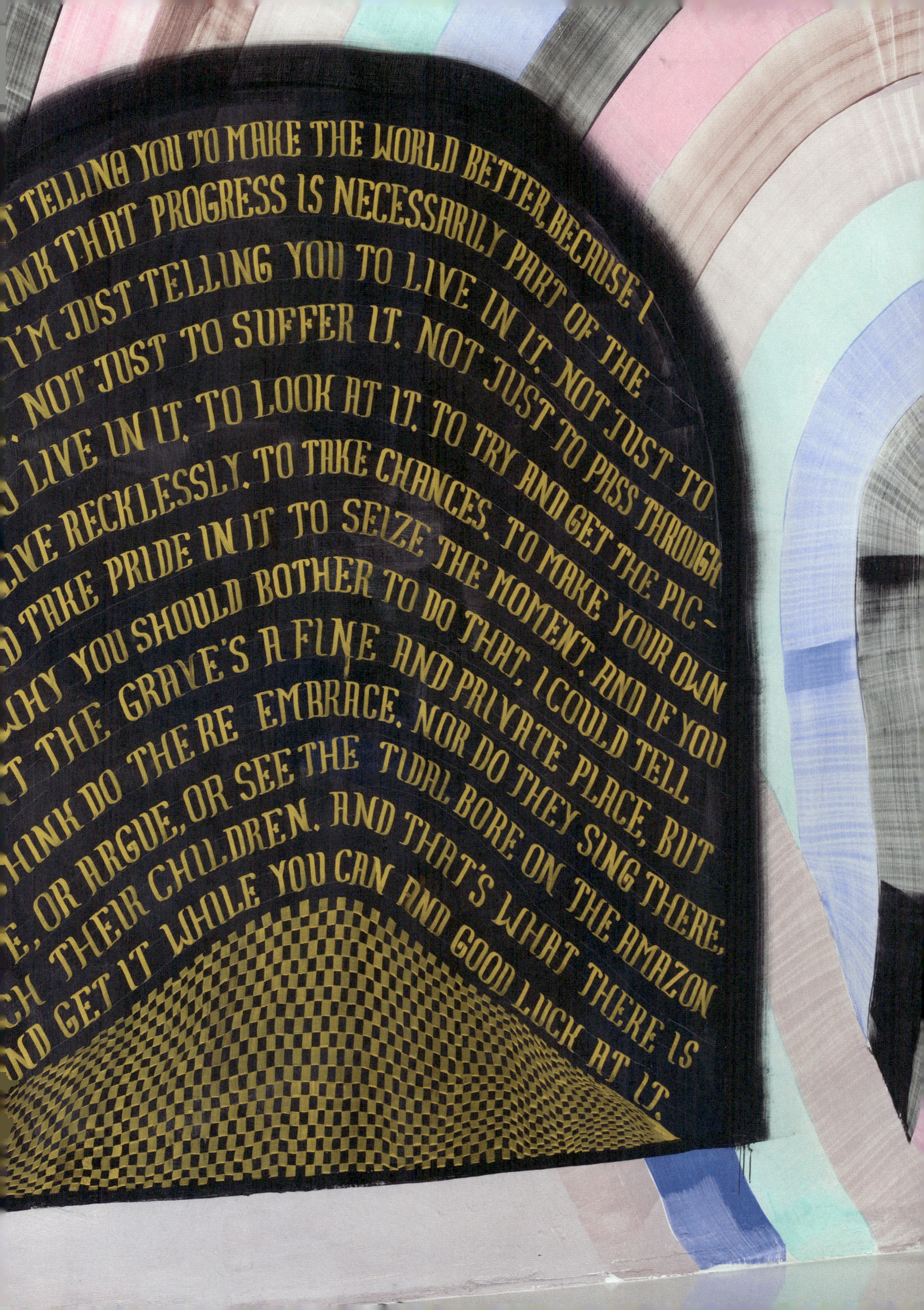

T TELLING YOU TO MAKE THE WORLD BETTER, BECAUSE I
INK THAT PROGRESS IS NECESSARILY PART OF THE
I'M JUST TELLING YOU TO LIVE IN IT. NOT JUST TO
, NOT JUST TO SUFFER IT. NOT JUST TO PASS THROUGH
LIVE IN IT. TO LOOK AT IT. TO TRY AND GET THE PIC-
LIVE RECKLESSLY. TO TAKE CHANCES. TO MAKE YOUR OWN
D TAKE PRIDE IN IT TO SEIZE THE MOMENT. AND IF YOU
WHY YOU SHOULD BOTHER TO DO THAT, I COULD TELL
T THE GRAVE'S A FINE AND PRIVATE PLACE, BUT
HINK DO THERE EMBRACE. NOR DO THEY SING THERE,
E, OR ARGUE, OR SEE THE TIDAL BORE ON THE AMAZON
CH THEIR CHILDREN. AND THAT'S WHAT THERE IS
ND GET IT WHILE YOU CAN AND GOOD LUCK AT IT.

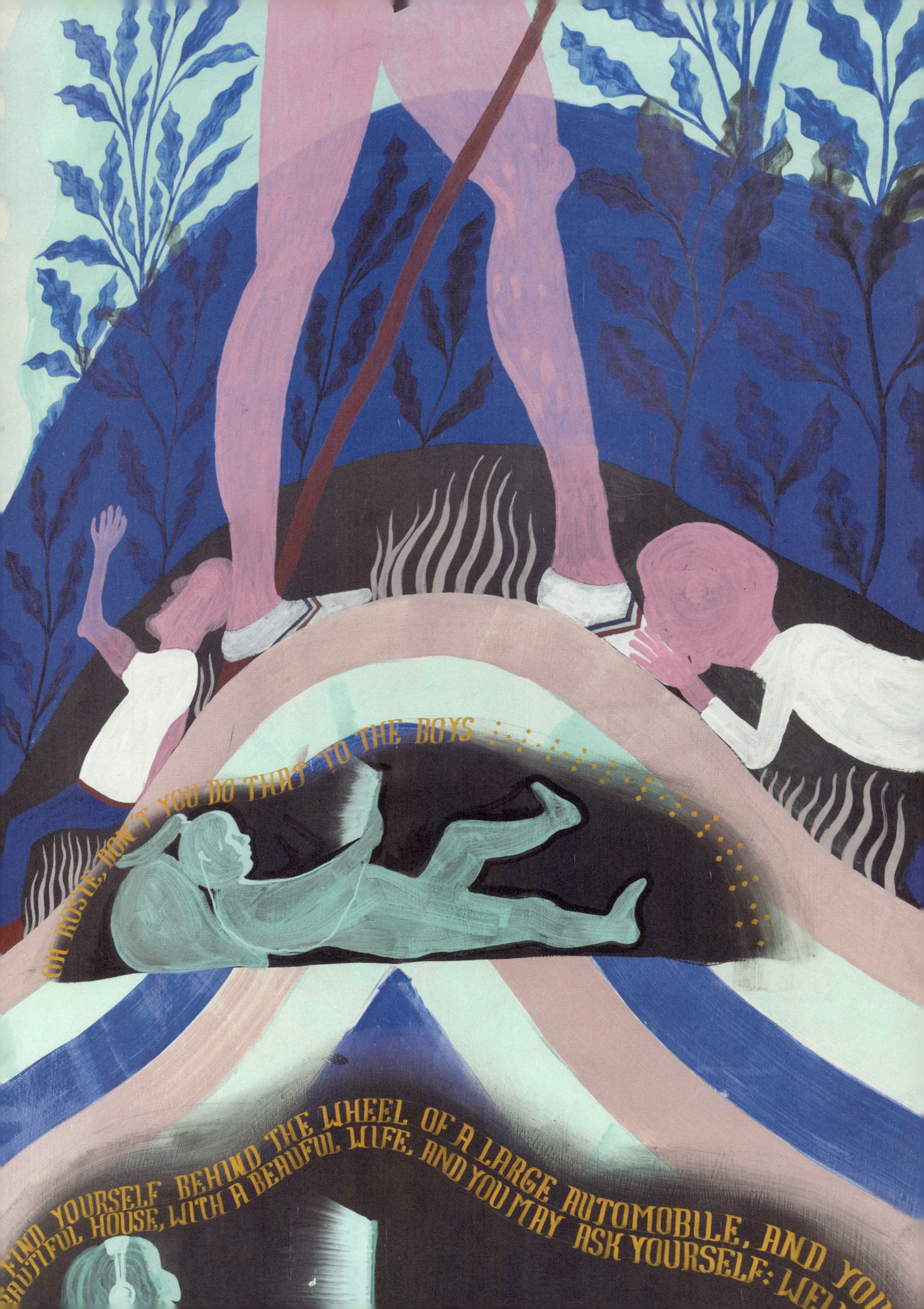
OH ROSIE, DON'T YOU DO THAT TO THE BOYS
FIND YOURSELF BEHIND THE WHEEL OF A LARGE AUTOMOBILE, AND YOU
AUTIFUL HOUSE, WITH A BEAUFUL WIFE, AND YOU MAY ASK YOURSELF:

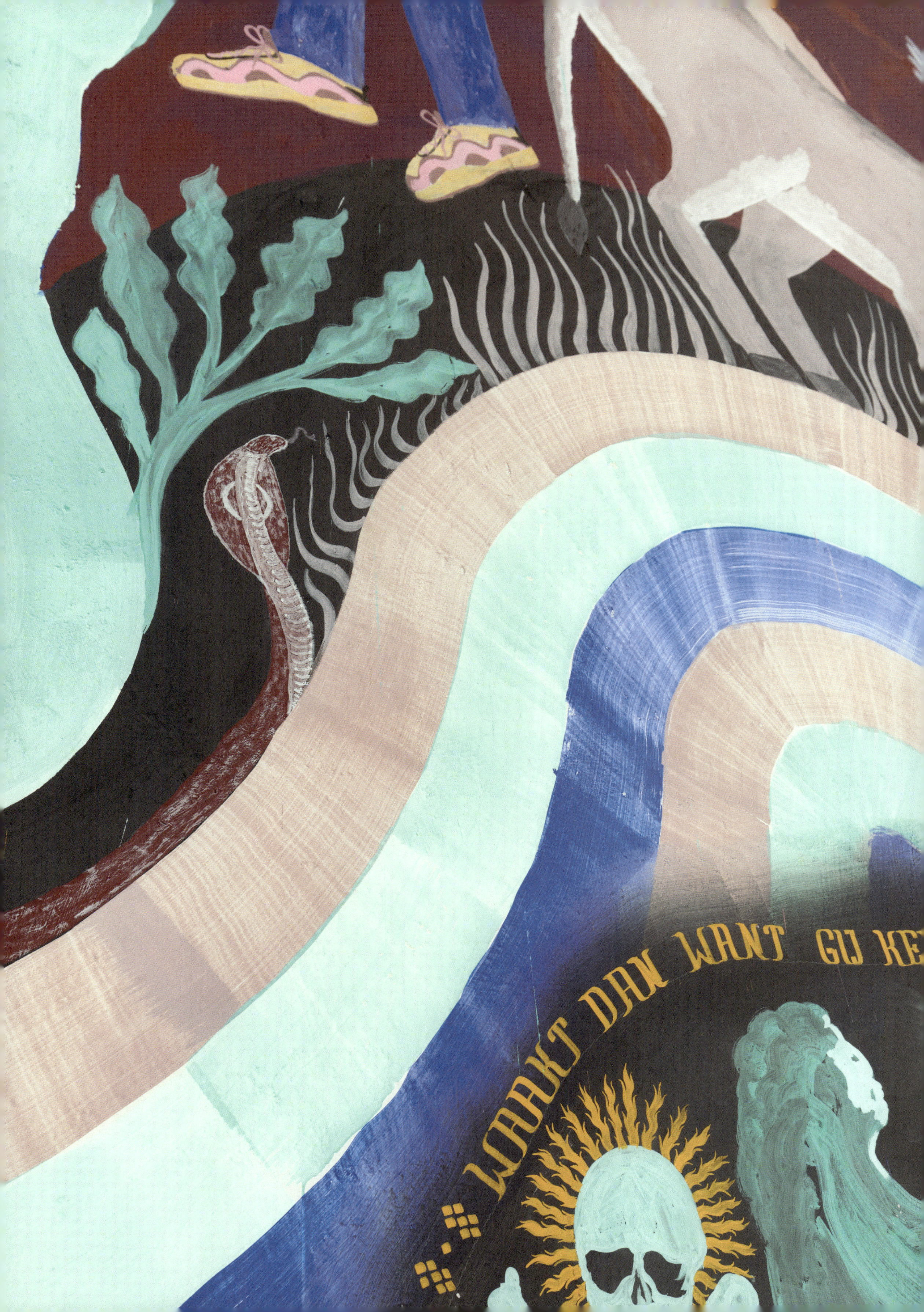
WAAKT DAN WANT GIJ

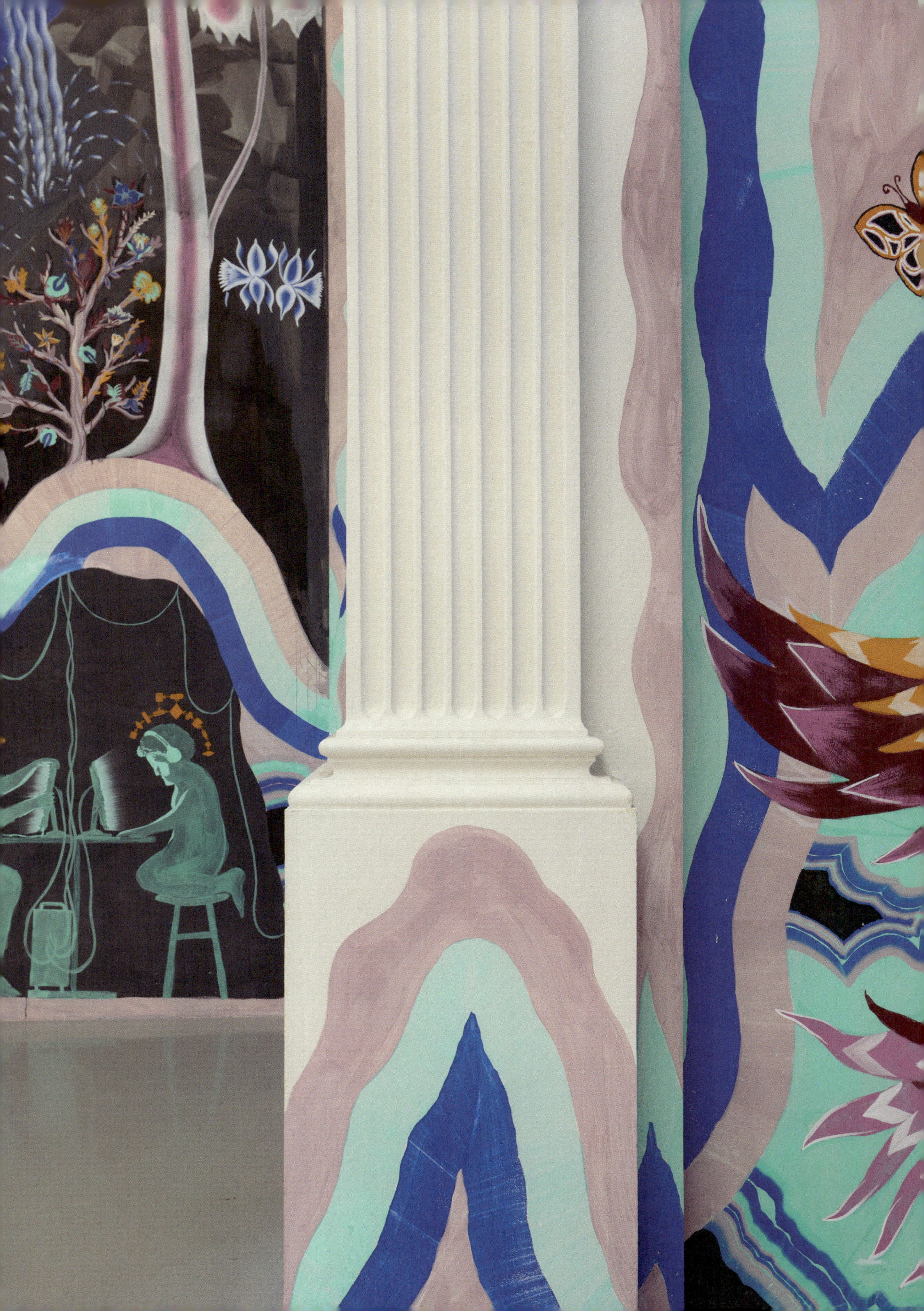

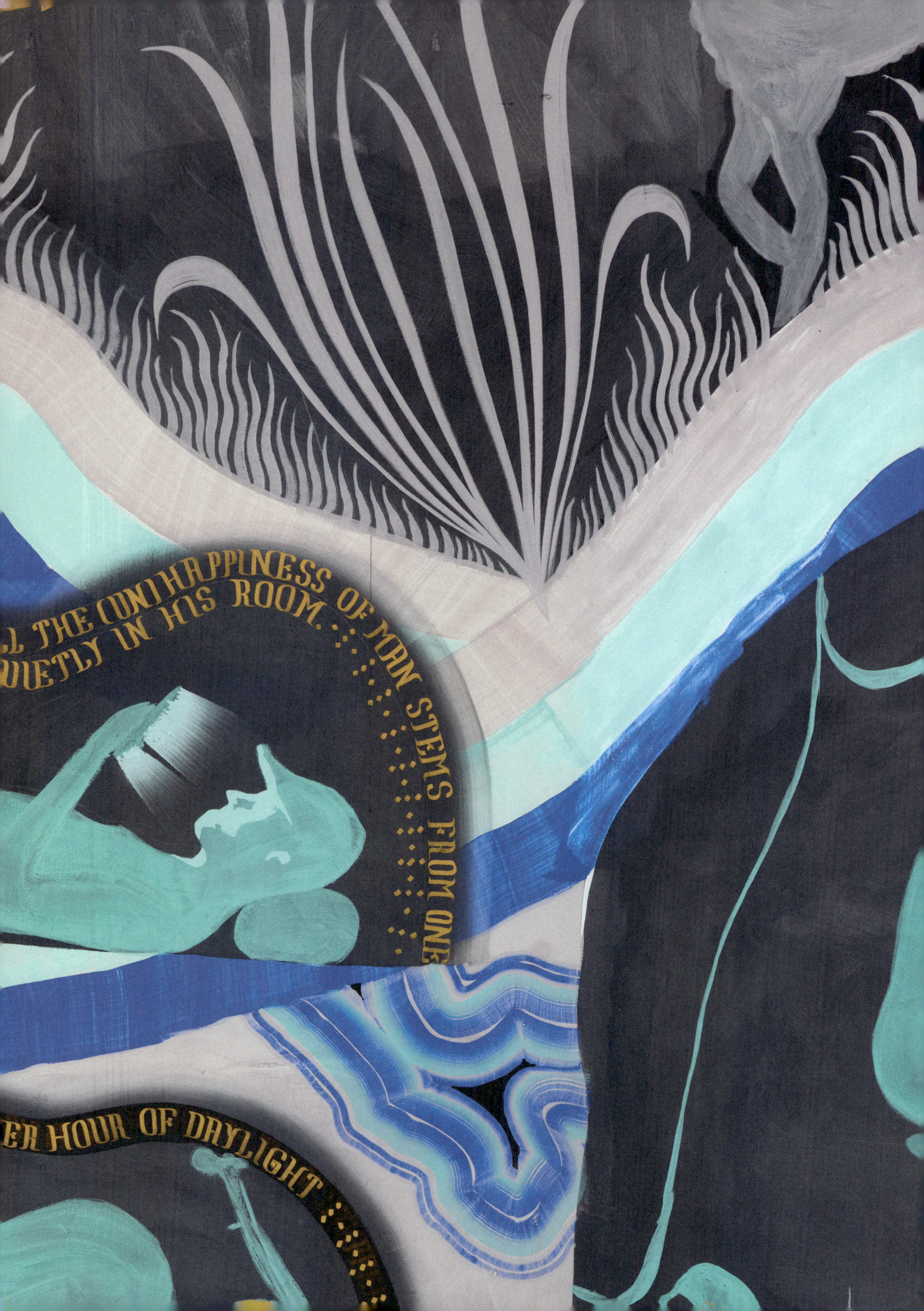
L THE (UN)HAPPINESS OF MAN STEMS FROM ONE
UIETLY IN HIS ROOM.
ER HOUR OF DAYLIGHT

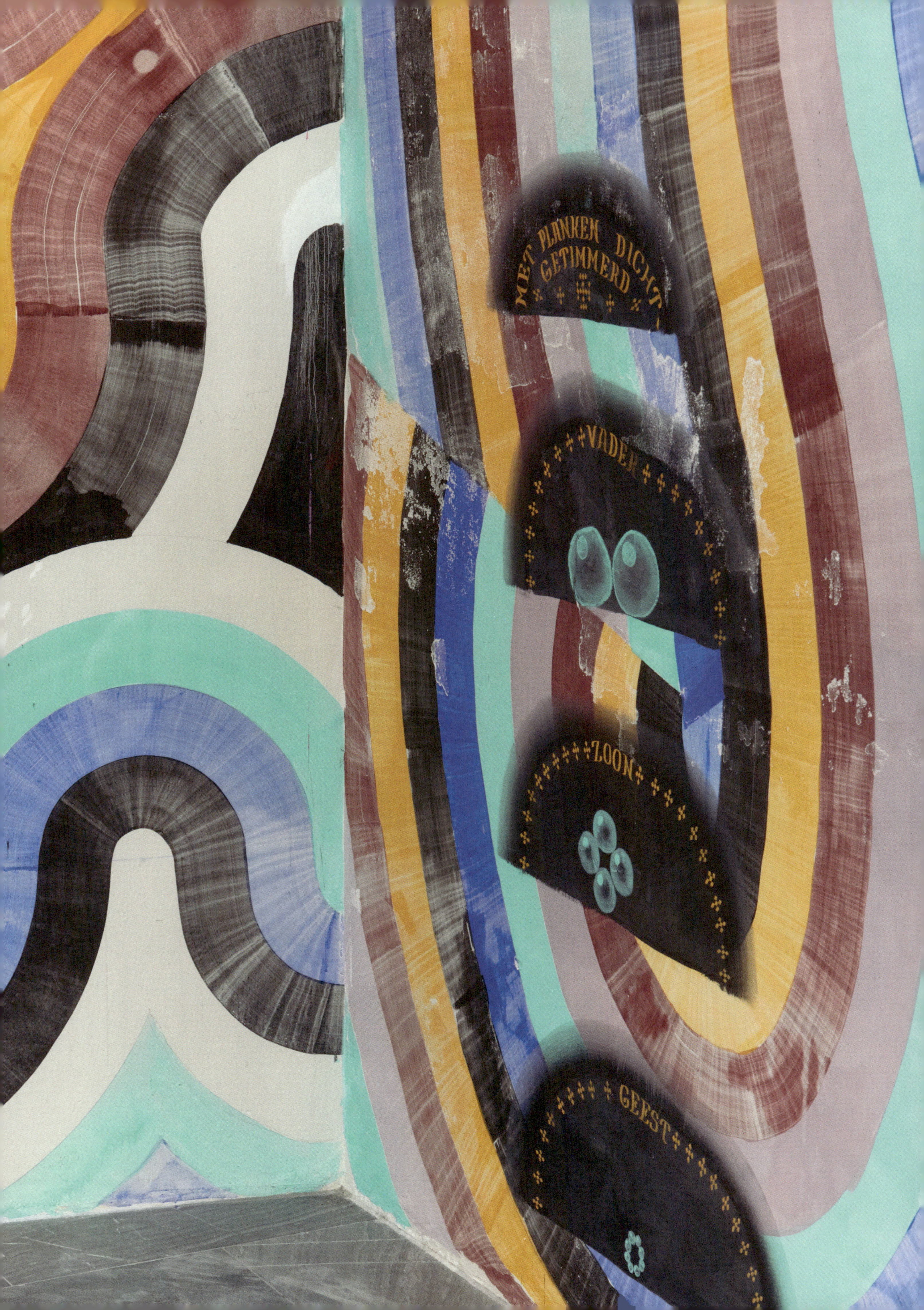
MET PLANKEN DICHT GETIMMERD
VADER
ZOON
GEEST

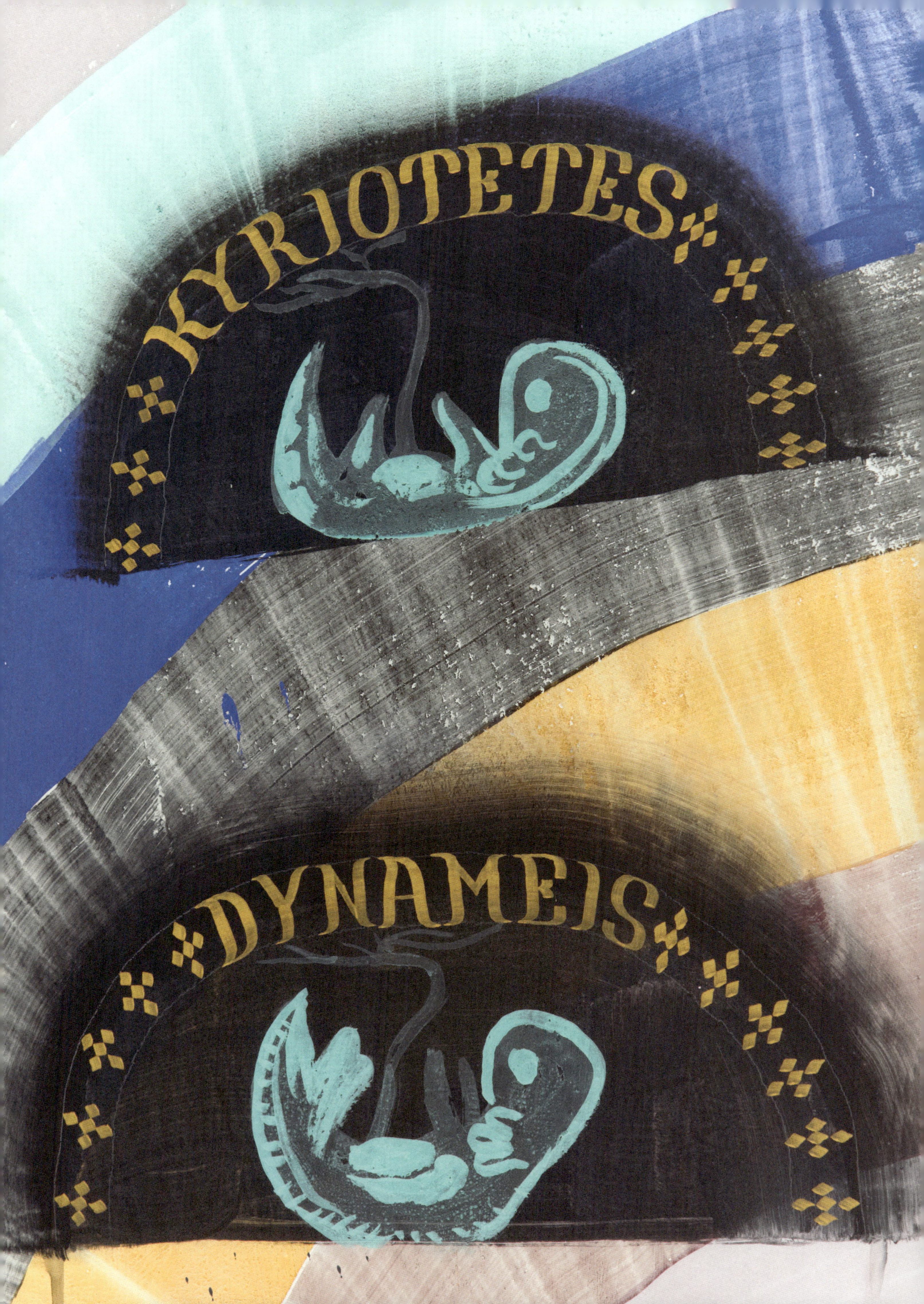
KYRIOTETES
DYNAMEIS

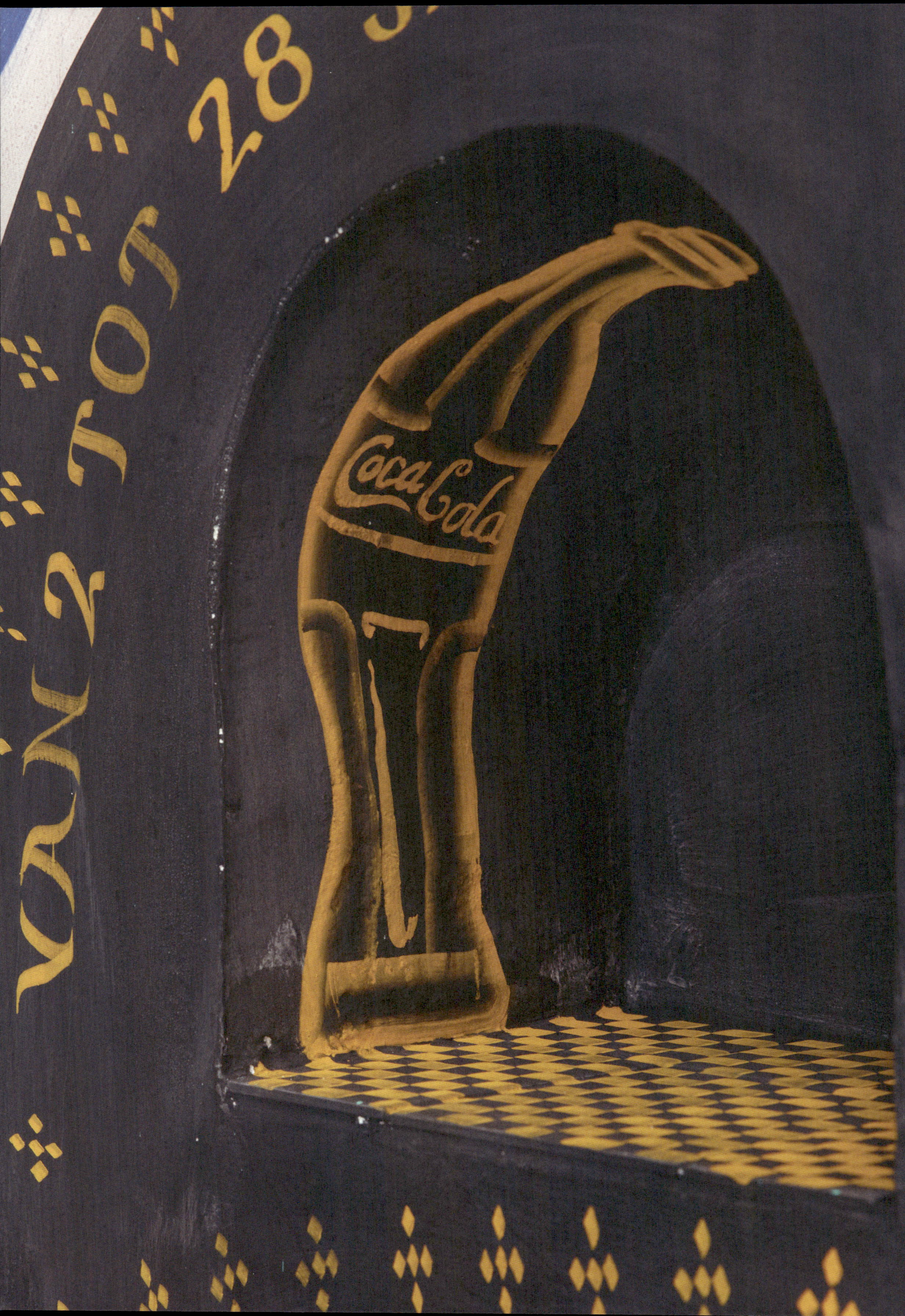
VAN 2 TOT 28
Coca-Cola

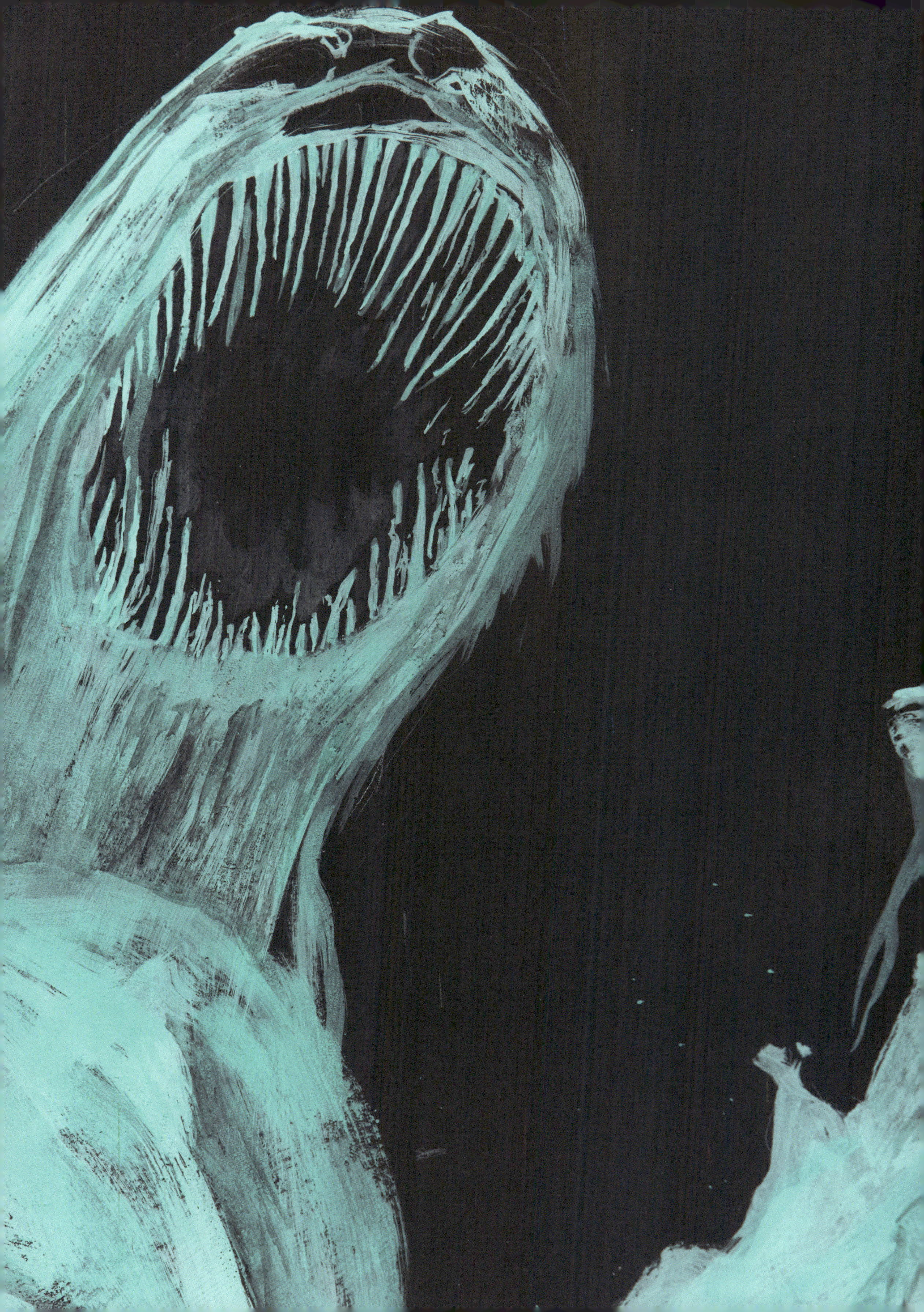

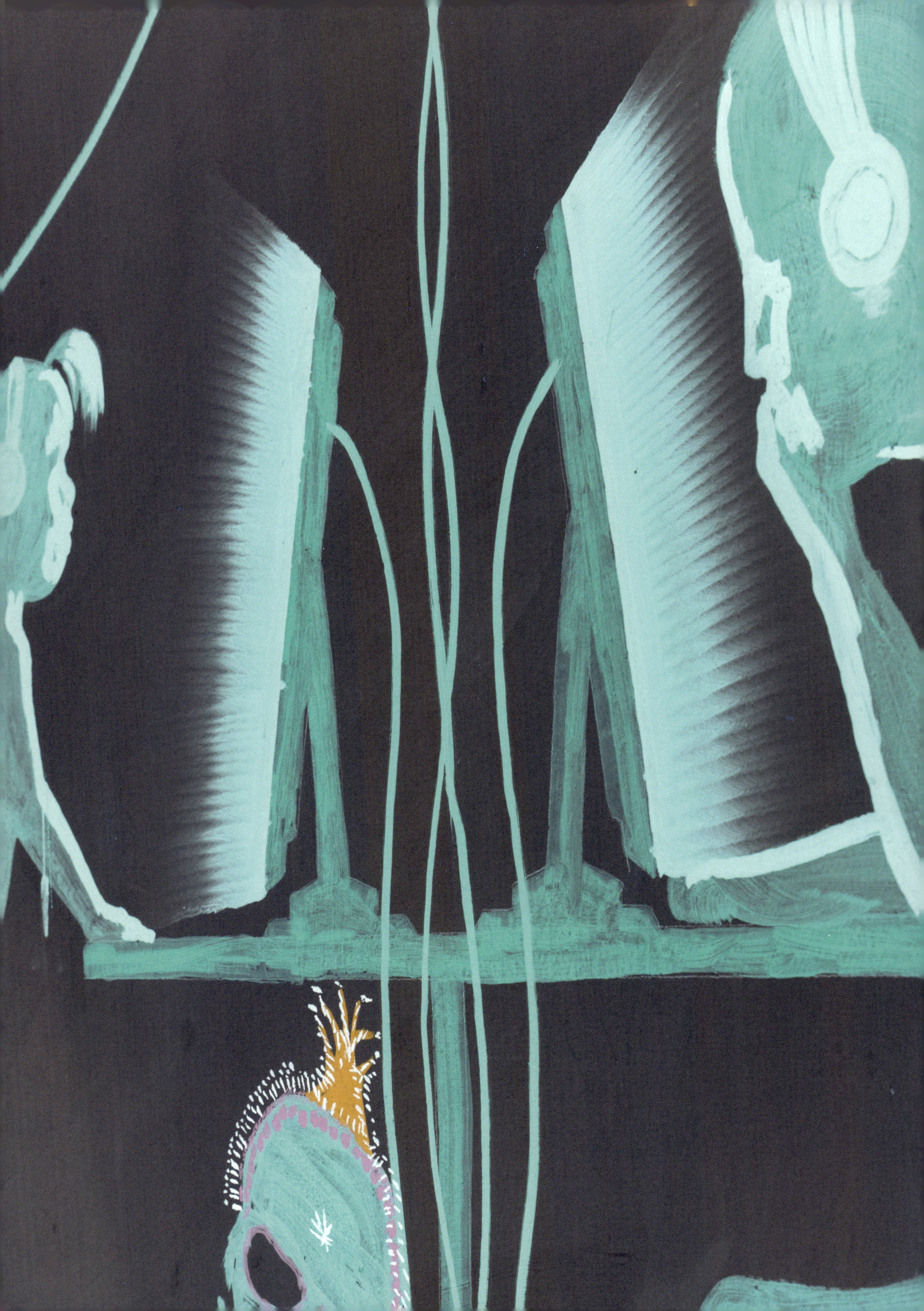

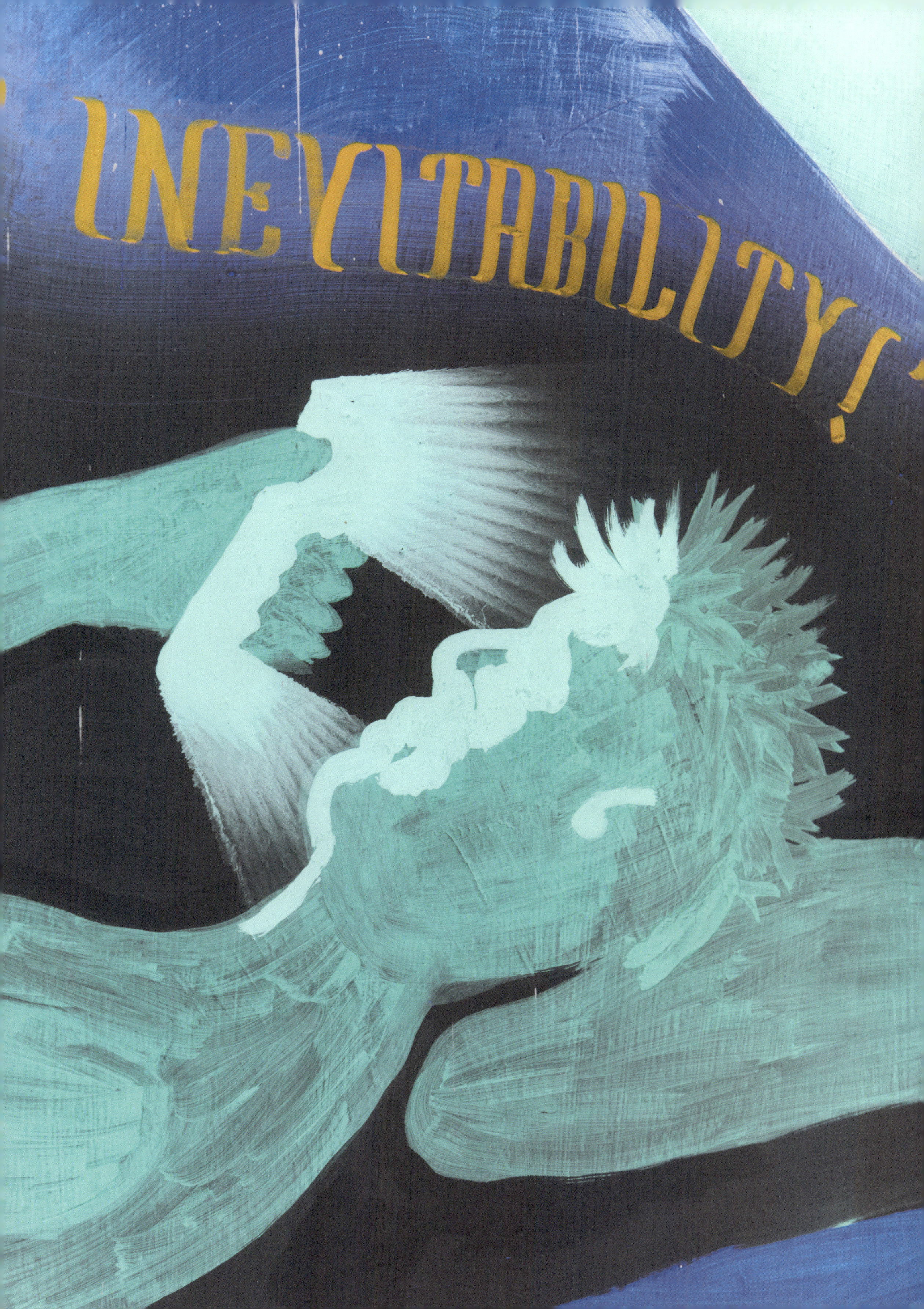
INEVITABILITY!

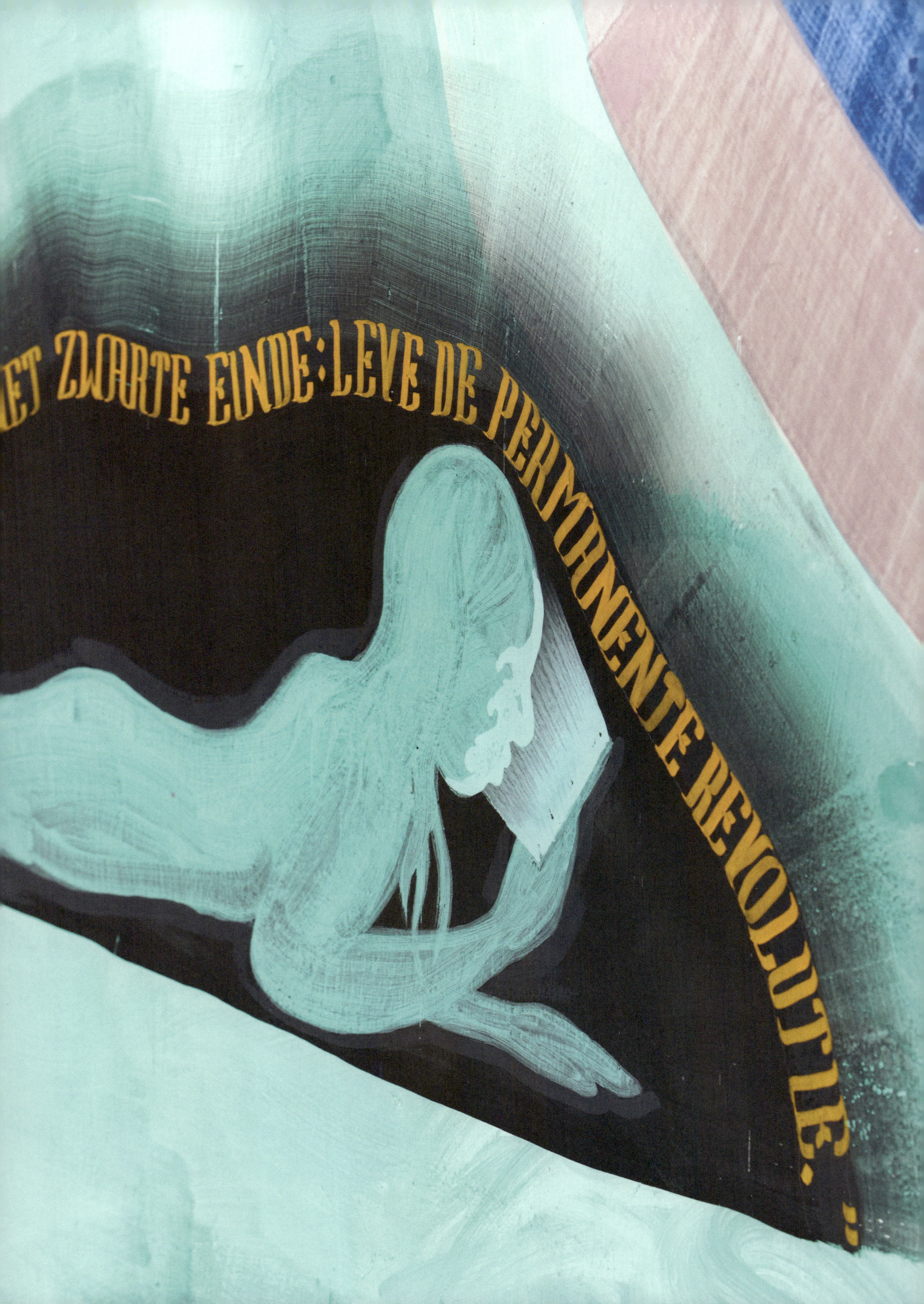
ET ZWARTE EINDE: LEVE DE PERMANENTE REVOLUTIE."

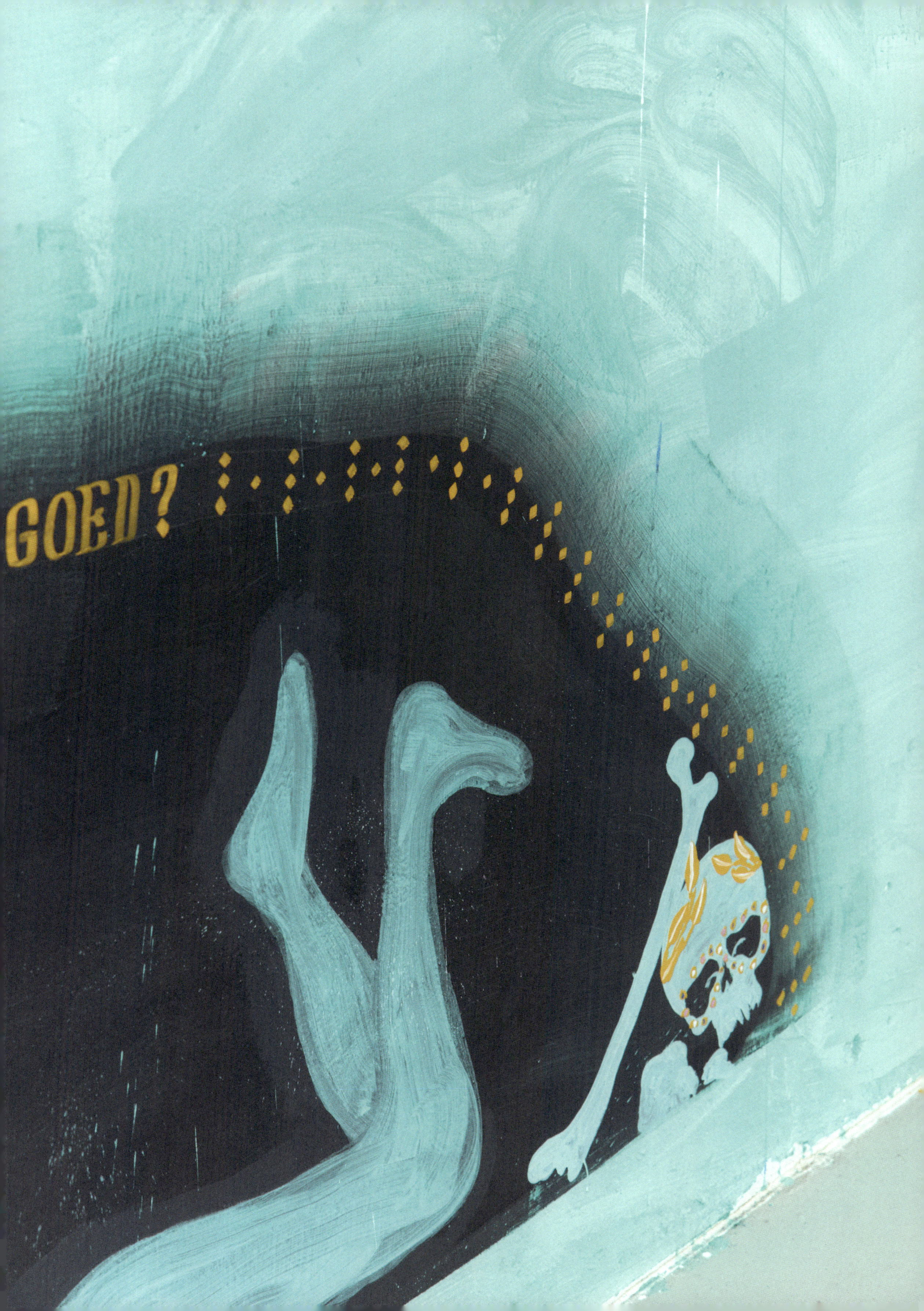
GOED?

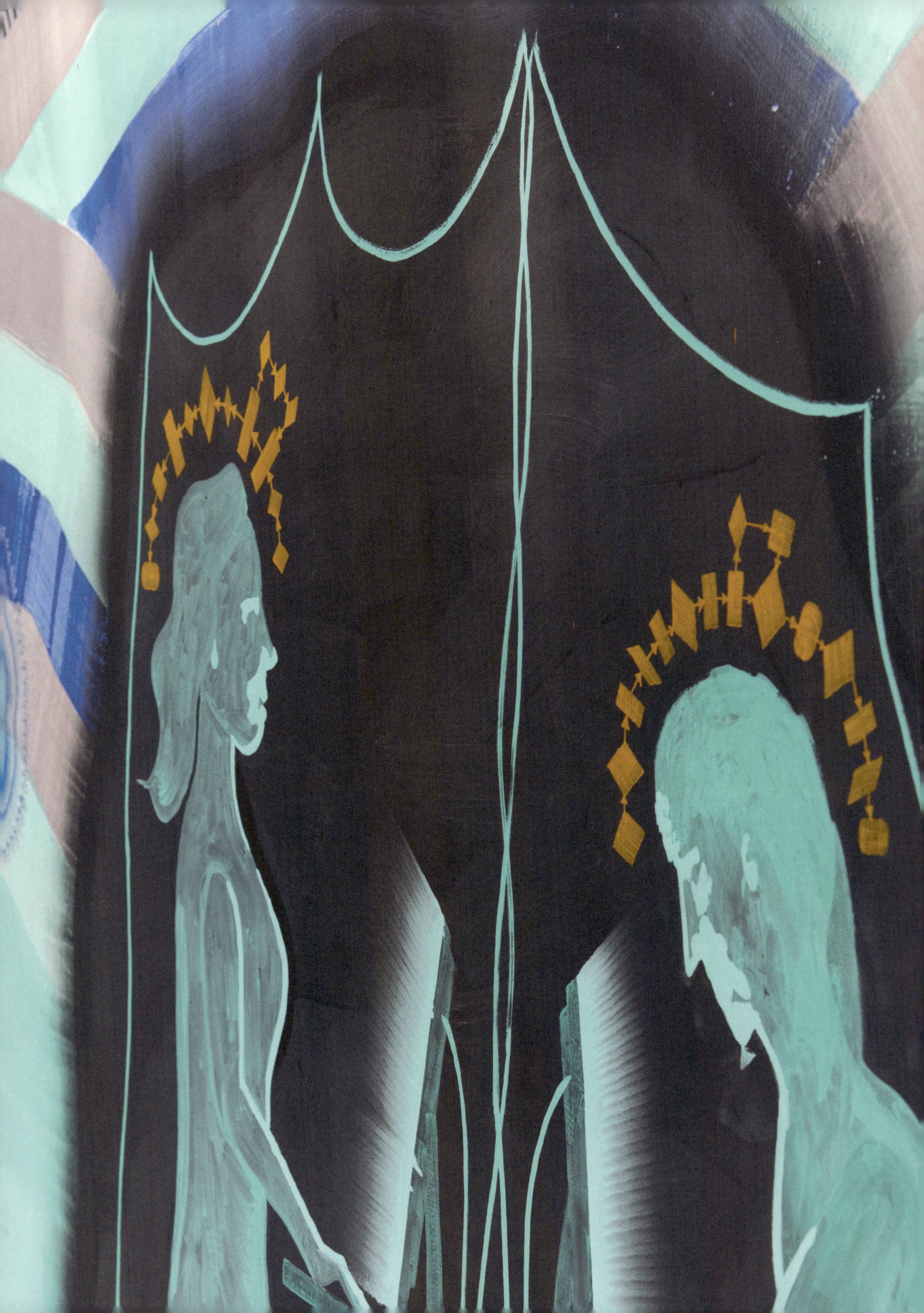

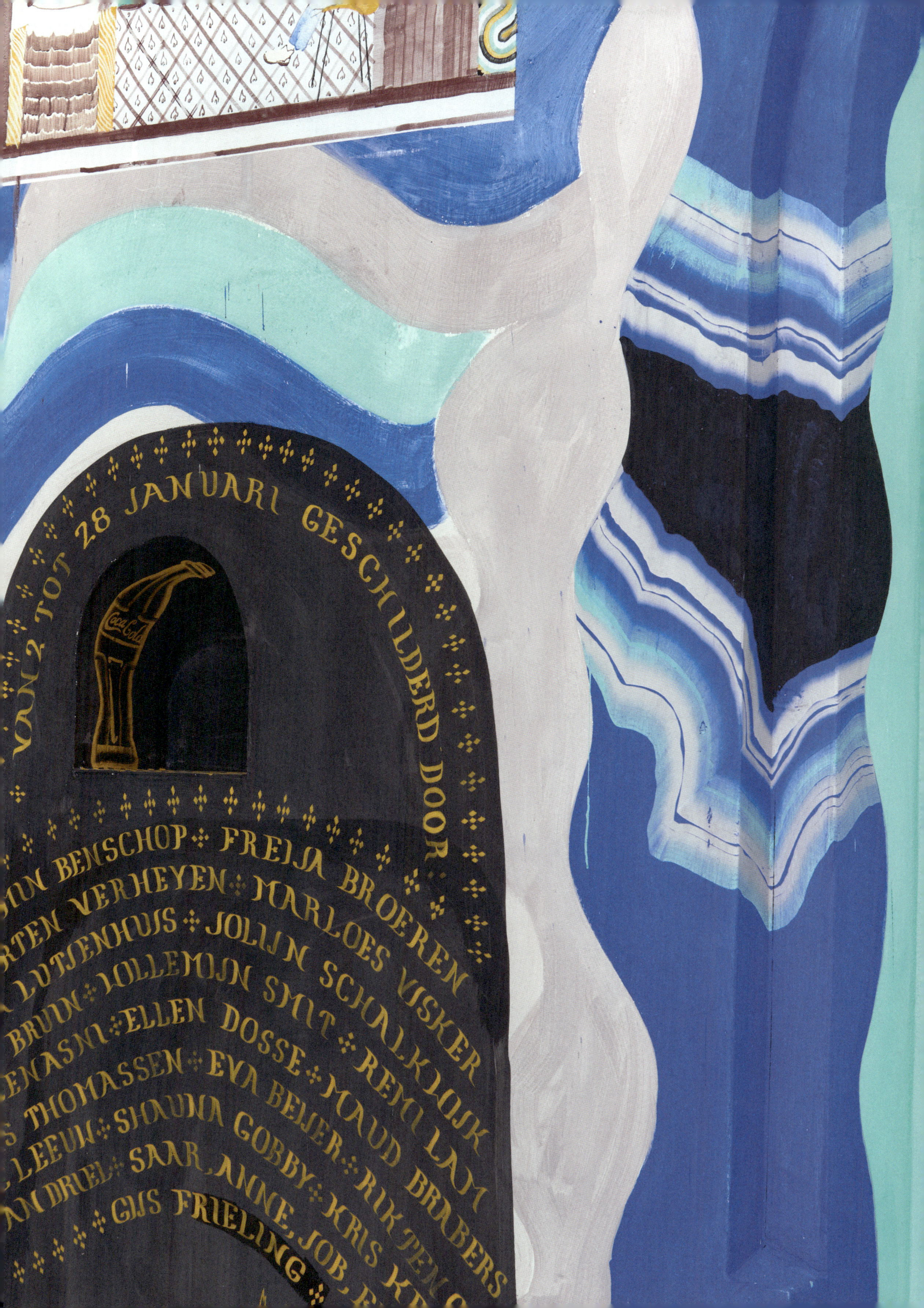
VAN 2 TOT 28 JANUARI GESCHILDERD DOOR:
Coca-Cola
BENSCHOP FREIJA BROEREN
VERHEYEN MARLOES VISKER
LUTJENHUIS JOLIJN SCHALKWIJK
BRUIJN LOLLEMIJN SMIT REMI LAM
ELLEN DOSSE MAUD BRABERS
THOMASSEN EVA BEIJER RIK TEN
LEEUW SHAUNA GOBBY KRIS
DRUEL SAAR, ANNE, JOB,
GIJS FRIELING

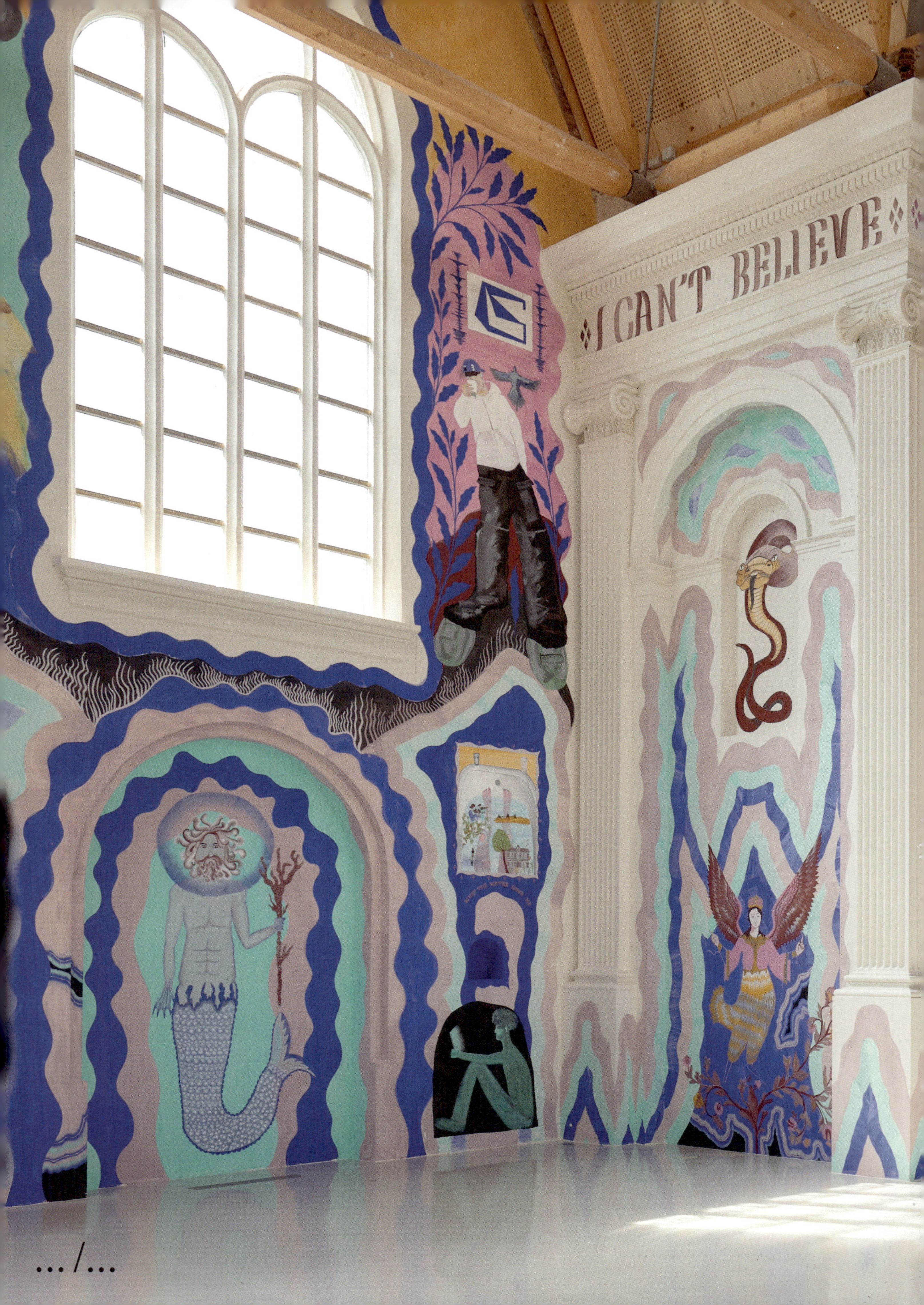
I CAN'T BELIEVE

…/…